The mysteries of life, of death, of injury and recovery, are beyond human intelligence. No individual can guarantee that tragedy will not strike or death will not call...

The Millers were a typical family who had lived through the usual quota of cuts and bruises, minor emergencies and challenges. But when a sudden accident left thirteen-year-old Kathy critically injured and fighting for her life, the Miller family was faced by trauma they had never before known.

Tragedy struck the Millers. But it did not defeat them. For they discovered the loving presence of a God who gives the ability to turn tragedy into triumph. KATHY is their story of victory.

Kathy

**BARBARA MILLER and
CHARLES PAUL CONN**

SPIRE BOOKS

Fleming H. Revell Company
Old Tappan, New Jersey

Scripture quotations in this volume are from the King James Version of the Bible.
Some of the names in this account have been changed.

Photographs by Jeffery R. Werner
© 1979 by Jeffery R. Werner

Library of Congress Cataloging in Publication Data

Miller, Barbara, date
    Kathy.

    1. Miller, Kathy.   2. Miller, Barbara, date
3. Methodists—United States—Biography.   4. Coma—
Biography.   I. Conn, Charles Paul.   II. Title.
BX8495.M527M54   287'.6'0922 [B]   79-93384
ISBN 0-8007-8415-4

To my family:
Larry, Larry Don, and Kathy,
for allowing me to share the greatest
gift I have—experiencing
the strength of Christ's love.

BARBARA MILLER

. . . and to Sharon, my sister.
Once, long ago, she too "came back,"
simply because God loves her,
as do I.

CHARLES PAUL CONN

Kathy

And we know that all things work together for good to them that love God, to them who are the called according to his purpose.

Romans 8:28

Chapter One

HE IS A quite ordinary man, middle-aged and respectable. He was driving home along a busy road in Scottsdale, Arizona, on a quite ordinary afternoon. What happened could have happened to anyone. It happened suddenly, without warning. Sam Hale tells it:

"I had been at work out at Cave Creek, north of Scottsdale. I was on my way home, sometime around four o'clock. I guess I was doing the speed limit. The traffic was heavy, two lanes going each way. It happened so quickly, so fast, it was just incredible. There were cars to the right of me; I was in the inside lane. All of a sudden, in a split moment, there were two girls darting out through traffic.

"It's the most vivid scene in my mind—those two girls. One turned and looked back my way. But the other one—the other one was looking the other way.

The first girl saw me and stopped, but not the other one. She just kept going; she just seemed to leap out in front of my car. I hit the brakes, and when I did, the car turned slightly and began to skid, just as I hit her. It was awful. She hit the fender on the passenger side and flew into the air. I remember her body coming over the front of the car.

"My car turned completely around and stopped, heading back the other way. I looked over, and there she was, lying there in the highway. It was obvious she was horribly hurt. She was lying there in some kind of fetal position. One of her legs stuck out at a disjointed angle.

"She was very quiet, very still. I was shaking. I was horribly frightened. I didn't know what to do—I was sure I had killed her."

* * * *

Dr. Jack Jewell is a gynecologist, and a good one. He lives in Carefree, Arizona, and was driving home that afternoon from his office in Scottsdale. He moved along with the rush-hour traffic, north on Scottsdale Road, finally leaving the downtown congestion and heading into the suburban desert area. He reached the intersection at Mescal Road:

"I came upon the accident moments after she was hit. I was one of the first to get out of a car. She was lying in the middle of the road, bleeding from the forehead. She was a twisted mess. I really wondered whether she was dead or alive. Her right leg was severely twisted, obviously fractured. Her neck was so twisted, I was afraid it was broken. I checked her pulse, and it was slow and weak, but it was steady. A crowd started to gather quickly, and I heard that an ambulance had been called.

"I used to drive an ambulance myself, back when I was in medical school. I've seen many cases like this. Many of them died, and died quickly. I would not have been surprised if she were dead on arrival at the hospital. I put in a call to the hospital for a neurosurgeon to be standing by. The child was unconscious; it was obvious she had severe head injuries.

"Why did I stop? Well, we physicians have mixed feelings about stopping at accidents. But, look, I'm a father. I've got four kids. Whether there was anything I could do or not, I thought it was imperative to stop and offer my services.

"Did I do anything to help her chances? Yes. I prayed. That's about all. Medically, there was nothing to do. But I prayed. And I told the ambulance boys, when they got her loaded, 'Boys, don't waste any time! Get her to the hospital!' Things looked pretty dark."

* * * *

March 14, 1977. It had been a slow day at Fire Station Number 12 in Scottsdale. The station is on Scottsdale Road, at the intersection of Thunderbird, only about one and one-quarter miles from Mescal, and houses three fire engines, each fully equipped for rescue and first aid. On duty there, around the clock, are paramedics called emergency medical technicians, in the official jargon of the department. Each paramedic works twenty-four hours on and twenty-four hours off. At the station that afternoon was Tim Hoffman, one day short of his twenty-third birthday, but already a four-year veteran of the department. He is a rugged, muscular young man, with dark, brooding good looks and a perpetually somber expression. He is a professional; he takes his work seriously:

"The call came across on an 'alert' monitor, from the radio dispatcher at the downtown station. It was a nine-sixty-two—accident with vehicle involved—and that's all we knew. I drove the truck; I was the duty engineer that day. We had an extremely fast response to that call—two or three minutes, at the most.

"When I arrived, there were probably five or six people out in the street. Traffic was backed up. The victim was right in the middle of the road. The car was off to the right. I pulled up right in front of her and blocked her body from the north. I pulled the truck within twenty-five or thirty feet of her.

"She was facedown. She had quite a bit of blood coming from her head. She had a severely angulated fracture of the leg. In a situation like that, we move the victim as little as possible. I got my equipment out and went over there. Dr. Jack Jewell was already there, plus a few other people. I said to one of them, 'I want everybody out of here, except Dr. Jewell!' One thing I just can't stand is gawkers; they just stand around and bother you. I started working on her, checking pulse, blood pressure, respiration.

"In my honest opinion, I didn't expect her to live

two more minutes. She was that bad off. I was expecting to have to work a 'full code.' That's when the victim's heart stops beating and respiration stops, due to extreme trauma. You have to anticipate the worst. Jewell said he was there to assist me, if I needed it, and I told him to stay by me, because I might need help. I expected her to go into full code any time. Her pulse was shallow, slow, weak.

"She had a severe compound fracture. The bone was exposed; the broken end had come through the skin at the back of the knee. I stabilized it in the position I found it in. We used a ladder splint, a metal splint about three inches wide. It's bendable, so it conforms to the position of the broken leg. We put one on each side of the leg and wrapped it, to stabilize it.

"She had been knocked out of her shoes. Her pants were ripped, so I covered her with a blanket. Soon after that, I think, her parents arrived, and there was nothing to do but wait for the ambulance to get there. I checked her pulse constantly. I tried to talk to her, and at first she moaned and sort of grunted, but after a few minutes, she stopped responding altogether. In my opinion, physically and medically speaking, I didn't see any possible way she could pull out of it."

* * * *

She was Kathryn Suzanne Miller, age thirteen—Kathy. She was a pretty, blonde eighth grader at Cocopah elementary school. She was a fine young athlete, a competitive swimmer and distance runner. And she was, of course, someone's daughter.

Chapter Two

No PARENTS can predict how they will react to a sudden tragedy like Kathy's accident.

Certainly Larry and I couldn't. We were typical parents, I suppose, and we had lived through the typical parents' quota of cuts and bruises, minor emergencies and challenges, with our two teenage children. But we had never faced this kind of trauma; and, like all parents, we really never thought we would. It was the kind of thing that always seems to happen to other people—the accidents that you read about in the paper. But who expects it to happen to themselves? Not us.

We were both home that Monday afternoon. Our sixteen-year-old, Larry, Jr., was at his high school's baseball practice. I came home from running a few errands at about four o'clock and found my husband, Larry, at the dining-room table. He was working as a marketing consultant for the Portland Cement Associa-

tion, and spent much of his time visiting various con-
struction sites around the Phoenix area. That day he
had come home early, to do paperwork and to make
some phone calls.

"Where's Kathy?" I asked.

"She just left a few minutes ago," Larry told me.
"She and Sheri [a neighborhood friend] went over to
the shopping plaza for a while."

Nothing unusual about that. I served Larry a bowl of
ice cream, and he went into the family room, sat down
in his favorite chair, and began reading papers he had
brought from the office. I was in the kitchen, cleaning
up the dishes, when the doorbell rang.

Before either of us had time to answer it, the door
flew open, and in burst Heidi, a girl who lived down
the block from us. "You gotta come quick!" she
blurted.

She was crying. I could tell by the look on her face
that something was badly wrong. I knew immediately
it had to be Kathy. "Kathy's been hit by a car on
Scottsdale Road!"

When she said Scottsdale Road, Larry and I both
had the same thought: The speed limit there is 45 miles
per hour, and the traffic is always fast and heavy.

There was no disguising Heidi's panic. As I ran to
the board where we hang our car keys, I immediately
started praying. I didn't have to be told that this was
terrible news—perhaps the most terrible news I had
ever received in my life. But I already felt a peculiar
calmness, and I found myself praying, "Okay, Lord,

what is my reaction supposed to be? Show me what to do, Lord. Tell me how to get through this."

We took my car, with Larry driving, and as we sped to the scene, less than a mile away, I prayed aloud for Kathy and asked God to prepare us for whatever we would find when we got to her. Larry says he remembers my praying for the driver of the car that hit her. I don't remember that, or much else, on the short ride to Scottsdale Road. As we turned onto the main road, we could see the crowd milling about, the police cars, the big, green fire truck pulled across the road. Larry ran a red light, passed a few cars, drove over the sidewalk, maneuvered as close as possible to the middle of the crowd, and we jumped out. I pushed through the people, wondering what I would find on the other side of that crowd.

My first sight was of Kathy's shoes, lying on the side of the road, and I thought, *Oh, my God, she was hit hard, to knock her out of her shoes!* She lay in a crumpled little heap, almost completely covered by a blanket. She was lying so very still that we thought she might already be dead. One little foot protruded from the bottom of the blanket, and a swatch of blonde hair was visible at the top. There was blood under her head. Her eyes were closed, and she was very pale and very still.

I went straight to her and knelt on my hands and knees on the pavement beside her. I believe in prayer, and I wanted to touch my daughter. I touched her limp left foot with my hand and prayed. As I touched her

foot, the most beautiful feeling I've ever had swept
my body. I had been aware of the presence of the Lord
many times before, but never like that. That time, it
was so different, because my need was so great. As I
prayed, all my fear was immediately removed. In-
stantly, I wasn't afraid anymore. A peace and quiet
flowed into me and over me. It was as if a bubble had
come down and encased us there on that pavement.
Even sounds were muted. I didn't hear the noise of the
cars in the street, or of the people. We were encapsu-
lated in calm and peace.

Somehow I knew that I had been in contact with the
Lord, that Kathy was in the hands of God, and things
were going to be all right. Immediately, my prayers
went from Kathy to Larry. I looked up at him. He was
a terrible gray color, and he looked tense and uptight.
He was a mess. I prayed for God to help Larry, to give
him the peace He was giving me. I looked around, at
the crowd of people lining the road. There was fear on
their faces; some of them were crying. I had a tremendous urge to go out and touch people and tell them
Kathy was going to be okay.

After that prayer, I stepped back from Kathy, and
the paramedic continued to work over her. There was
a man there with him, who I later learned was a doctor
who had stopped to help. Neither of them said very
much as we waited for the ambulance to arrive. A man
named Herb Drinkwater, the proprietor of a wine-
and-cheese shop nearby, tried to reassure us. Kathy's
pulse was regular, he said, and her blood pressure was

stable. We asked him to call our family doctor and have him meet us at the hospital, and he did so.

People have asked me if I confronted the driver in any way at the scene of the accident. I didn't. I knew he must have been there, but I never asked to see him, and to this day, I don't know what he looks like. I was vaguely aware of the police chalking off the tires of a late-model automobile, and remember thinking that must be the car that hit her.

When the ambulance arrived, the paramedic slid a large, flat sheet of plywood under Kathy, to lift her onto the stretcher, and then moved her into the back of the ambulance. I rode up front with the driver; Larry and the fire-department paramedic rode in the back with Kathy. Just before we pulled away, the doctor who had been helping told us that Kathy had a bad head injury and that he would call ahead for a neurosurgeon to be standing by. Then, quickly, as if not to alarm us, he asked a final question: Were we Protestant or Catholic? "Protestant," Larry mumbled. The implication was clear and unmistakable. Kathy was at the verge of death, and the race to the hospital was to be a race for life itself.

* * * *

A tension-filled ambulance. Rush-hour traffic. A thirty-minute ride, with sirens wailing and cars and pedestrians flashing by outside the window. It was a wild, unreal scene. But, ironically, that chaotic setting gave Larry a place to think, a place where the most basic values in his life came suddenly into sharp focus.

He sat in the back of the ambulance beside Kathy; occasionally he would call her name, trying to get some response from her. There was nothing, not even a moan or a flicker of an eyelid. The paramedic constantly monitored her heartbeat and blood pressure. The ambulance lurched and jerked, as it made its way through the traffic.

Larry sat helplessly, with nothing to do but look down at her pale, still face, his thoughts tumbling through his mind. He kept thinking the whole scene was some sort of nightmare, that he would eventually wake up from it all. Then the crackle of the ambulance radio would bring him back to reality. He heard himself pulling for her to hang on until we got to the emergency room. "Just hold on, Kathy. Everything's going to be all right," he said, over and over. And as he spoke the words, he realized how everything else that had seemed so important a couple of hours before—the problems at his job, the bills to pay, business deals to make—all those things became totally insignificant. Nothing else in the world mattered, except the life of his little girl. If she would keep breathing, keep living, nothing else in the world would matter. He looked down at her and could think only of that happy little kid who had run out his front door an hour earlier, giggling and bubbly, full of life.

I was in the front seat and started a vigil of prayer. I had felt that peace from God as I knelt on the busy road, and I was determined not to let it go. I began thanking God for all the good things, thanking Him for the positive things. I tried to praise Him for letting

Larry be at home with me, glad that I wasn't alone when it happened. I thanked Him that all these people seemed to know what they were doing, that the paramedic and ambulance had come so quickly, that the cars were pulling over to let us by.

I remember praying, "Lord, I thank You in advance that You're going to give me the presence of mind to know who to call when we get to the hospital and that You'll surround us with people who will support us."

We were really moving rapidly through traffic, as we neared the congested downtown area. We began having trouble getting through. As we neared the intersection at Indian School Road, we found ourselves approaching five lines of traffic, all backed up. The driver headed into the intersection very fast. It looked as if there were no possible way to get through. The paramedic yelled at the driver, and he slammed on the brakes. I prayed, "Lord, part the cars and let us through." For a moment, it looked as if we wouldn't make it. Then, somehow, at the last moment, the cars separated just enough for us to squeeze through. *Praise the Lord!* my heart shouted. The ambulance swerved and rocked and threw everyone forward, then turned left and headed down a side street, toward the hospital.

"I didn't see any way we could have gotten through," the paramedic told Larry. "I thought we had hit. I guess the ambulance must have rocked just enough to miss those cars. I'll tell you—we were just lucky."

But I had another explanation. I would wait until a

better time to give it, but I definitely knew that what guided that ambulance was something far greater than luck. We reached the doors of the emergency room at 5:05 P.M. A team of doctors and nurses was waiting for us as we pulled up. As the attendants wheeled the stretcher through the doors, only one thing seemed important to Larry and me: Kathy Miller was still alive.

Chapter Three

I WAS SURPRISED to realize, as we entered the hospital, that I was *not* a complete wreck. I felt calm and steady, almost as if I were moving with a power not my own. They wheeled Kathy into the emergency room. I had to give all the necessary information at the front desk: social-security numbers, insurance contacts, that sort of thing. I filled out all those forms, then went to a telephone and made four or five calls, to the people who needed to know about Kathy. The numbers came into my mind almost as if Someone were dictating them to me.

It could be, I suppose, that I was in a state of semishock—that I was still stunned and numb. But I don't believe that. I believe God was already there with me, giving me strength to meet my need. There was beginning a long chain of small incidents, by which God reminded me that He was by my side.

Larry and I waited in a small area outside the emergency room. The hospital staff was matter-of-fact and totally efficient. They went about the job quickly and quietly: making X rays, cleaning away the blood and dirt, and attaching monitoring devices to Kathy's body. We saw doctors come and go. A nurse emerged from the room and gave me a necklace, a ring, and a single earring that Kathy had been wearing. The tension built.

Kathy's friends, young teenage girls, began arriving: A small, huddled group of them formed in the hall. They became very emotional, crying and obviously afraid. I got up from where I sat and took them all to a small room down the hall, and there we had prayer. I told them that God had showed me that Kathy was in His hands and that things were going to be all right. I shared, for the first of what would be hundreds of times, the peace that God had given me, and asked the girls to join me in a prayer of thanks, a prayer of positive affirmation. After we prayed, I gave Kathy's jewelry to a girl named Janet, her closest friend, and said, "Wear this in faith until Kathy comes home again." And when I said it, I truly believed that it would come to pass. The tears began to dry.

After what seemed a long wait, the neurosurgeon came into the hall to meet us. His name was Dr. Fred Christensen, and he had been summoned to the emergency room by the first radio call from the scene of the accident. He was a young man, with that brisk, clinical tone of physicians who have bad news to give.

He was intense, unsmiling. "Your daughter has a very bad brain injury," he began. "There is some brain stem involvement, the extent of which I am uncertain." He stopped.

But how is she, we wondered? We wanted something more than that—some simple message to tell us she was going to be well again.

He hesitated, then responded: "Right now, she is in guarded condition." Another pause. We waited, almost without breathing. "All I can tell you is that it's very bad, and she may not make it through the night. If she does, we'll look at the next twenty-four hours. For the next three days, we just won't know. The next few days will be critical."

And with that, he left. It was not much to hang on to, but it was all we had, and we would live with it. Kathy was alive, at least for the moment; but there were no guarantees for tomorrow or the next day or the next.

I went looking for her. She had been removed from the emergency room and was being prepared for surgery on her leg. I stuck my head into the room where I thought she might be, and saw a woman's naked body lying on a table. The woman was obviously a mature adult, and I thought, *That can't be Kathy,* and hastily backed out of the room. I moved down the hall, still looking for her. When finally I found her, she *was* that young woman lying in the first room I had tried—the one with the woman's body, who had looked so unlike my little girl. It gave me a

jolt. I had not even recognized her. When your children are young, you know every bump on their
bodies, every scratch, every new wrinkle. But Kathy,
my baby, had been growing up right under my nose,
and I hadn't even recognized her. *Give me a chance,
Lord, to see my little girl become a woman,* I breathed in
prayer.

They wheeled her away, first to work on her leg,
then to a bed in the intensive-care unit. The orthopedic
surgeon came by, to say that her leg was badly broken
and would be put in traction and require additional
surgery later. "But let's think about the brain, primar-
ily, right now," he told us.

One of Kathy's young friends came to the hospital in
that first couple of hours, walked up to Larry, crying,
and gave him Kathy's shoe. She had picked it up off
the highway. It was just an old, scruffy, suede shoe,
but somehow it was more than Larry could take. As he
held it in his hand, he broke down and cried for the
first time. At a time like that, a dirty old shoe (one of
those new-style shoes, which he had always thought
so ugly) seemed so important to Larry because it represented Kathy. It *was* Kathy. Seeing that shoe broke him
up, and he stood in the hospital hallway, clutched it in
both hands, and cried. He disappeared after that, and
later I learned that he had gone to the hospital chapel
to pray.

My thoughts turned to Larry, Jr., who had been
practicing with his high-school baseball team at the
time of the accident. I went to a hospital phone and

called the school. No answer. I found the number of the baseball coach's office and dialed it, but had no luck there, either. I was desperate to talk to him, and I had no way to reach him. As happened so frequently on that long afternoon, I felt an edge of panic creep through me: What could I do, to get a message to Larry, Jr.? I closed my eyes and started to pray. As I did, the big, steel double doors clanked open behind me. I turned around, and in he walked. We embraced, and he told me that a neighbor had heard about the accident and gone to the ball field to get him. He had been told Kathy had a broken leg, so he arrived laughing and unconcerned, expecting to crack a few jokes with his little sister, to be with her, and help take her mind off what he thought was a minor injury. We told him the truth about her condition. Then, together, we waited.

* * * *

Kathy spent the night in the hospital's intensive-care unit. We were allowed in to see her for a ten-minute visit every two hours. There was no way to communicate with her, of course, and nothing to do but stand at the side of the bed and and look at her, but those brief visits were all we had, and they became precious to us. We stayed that first two nights and days in the waiting area of the ICU, pacing the floor, occasionally falling into an uneasy sleep in the chairs, waiting through the virtually endless two-hour periods, to get those ten minutes at Kathy's bedside.

We talked to her, hoping she could perhaps hear.

"C'mon, Kathy. Wake up, honey. We're here with you, Kathy." We stroked her arms and hair. She had a frightening assortment of devices attached to her, all types of monitors, keeping track of various body functions. She was lying on a thermal blanket; her right leg was in traction, suspended above the bed's surface by a set of iron weights. As the first night wore on, her breathing became labored and heavy; she struggled with each breath, sucking air noisily through clenched teeth, as if fighting for air. A nurse explained to us that this "brain-stem breathing" was common for victims of severe brain damage, but to us it was a heartbreaking sight, just the same. It was our Kathy, fighting for her life, and we could only stand helplessly by her bed and watch.

About 2 A.M. that first night, during one of our ten-minute visits at her bedside, we were trying to talk to Kathy. Larry and I each held one of her hands. "Kathy, can you hear me?" I said, close to her ear. In retrospect, that may seem foolish, but at the time, I was determined to try to get through to her, and I persisted. Maybe I had seen it work in the movies. All I know is that it seemed worth trying. "Kathy," I spoke, slowly and distinctly, "if you can hear me, *squeeze my hand.*"

At just that moment, ever so slightly, we felt a squeeze. Larry and I looked at each other across the bed. "Did you feel that?" I asked him, excitedly. He had felt it, too! I immediately ran for a nurse, to tell her the news.

Almost before I could blurt it out, the nurse quietly but emphatically burst our bubble. "Don't even think that," she scolded me. "In the condition your daughter is in, a squeeze of the hand is purely an involuntary reflex. It means absolutely nothing." She looked at Larry, then back to me, making sure we both received the full weight of her meaning. "It's wrong for you to even hope, at this point," she concluded softly. With that, she was gone.

We were crushed. I walked wearily back out to the waiting area, lay down on a couch, covered up with a blanket, and asked the Lord in prayer, "Why? Why, Lord? Why would the nurse respond that way? Why would she be so quick to take away that one little flicker of hope?" And the answer seemed to come back to me from God Himself: "You are not to seek answers from the nurses and doctors, because they don't have the answers. Only I have the answers. Kathy is in My hands. A miracle is being done, and only I know. Don't ask the medical people about Kathy. Ask Me."

And with that came the same peace and hope that I had felt at the scene of the accident. I got the message; after that night, I was determined to lean entirely on the Lord. I had no way of knowing what lay ahead, and, at that point, it was probably a very great blessing that I didn't. "Okay, Lord," I prayed, "from now on, my answers are coming from You." And slowly, fitfully, I dozed off to sleep.

Chapter Four

BARBARA MILLER insists that her family is an average family, an ordinary family, and in a sense she is right about that. They are indeed typical in many ways: early middle-aged parents with teenage son and daughter, middle-sized house with a middle-sized mortgage in the suburbs, all the usual concerns and interests of the average American household.

But, in other ways, the Millers are not ordinary at all. Certainly not now; not after living through the extraordinary experiences surrounding Kathy's accident. Such a crisis as they have had tends to test and eventually improve the mettle of a family, and the Millers of 1980 are in that sense not at all ordinary. As is so often in the case of such family emergencies, they have been through some things most of us have not, and as a result they are different from the average family. And even before the accident, the Millers were not as typical as Barbara might believe. They were for many years a baseball family, following the trail of Larry's fortunes as a professional pitcher in the major and minor leagues.

Larry Miller was a strong-armed left-hander who, like so many boys growing up in the Midwest, "played baseball all my life." A star in the sandlot and American Legion leagues as a youngster, he went to the University of Kansas on a baseball scholarship and had a couple of great years there, making the all-star team of the Big Eight Conference as a sophomore and a junior. After his junior year (10 wins and 2 losses as a starting pitcher), he signed a professional contract with the Los Angeles Dodgers and began his career in their minor-league farm system.

In his last semester at the University of Kansas, he met an attractive, red-haired member of the freshman class named Barbara Barlow, a speech-therapy major. They dated, married, and almost immediately moved far from home, on the professional baseball circuit. Larry was the property of the Dodgers, and wherever they sent him, he went, with Barbara (and eventually little Larry, Jr., and Kathy) by his side. First stop: Macon, Georgia, for the 1960 season. Then he went to Atlanta, to play for the Atlanta Crackers, then a half-season in Greenville, South Carolina. Larry had graduated from the ROTC Unit at the University of Kansas, and was on active reserve duty while playing baseball. When the famous Berlin crisis occurred in 1962, President John Kennedy, in a show of United

States military strength, activated several army reserve units, and Larry's number came up. He was ordered to Fort Sill, Oklahoma, for two years of active duty as an artillery instructor. That was two long, barren years of enforced absence from baseball. For a professional athlete, it was like stealing two years from his life, even though the addition of a baby girl named Kathy during that time helped make Fort Sill a pleasant memory for him.

Larry's discharge came in 1964, just in time for spring training. By this time he was twenty-six years old, and younger pitchers dominated the attention of the Dodger coaches. It was a frustrating spring for him, and when the regular season started, he was sent to the Albuquerque Dukes, an AA team in the Dodger system. Even there, he was put on the bench, rarely getting a chance to pitch, even in relief, and never able to show that he could still produce as a starter. He was discouraged—so discouraged that he almost decided to quit baseball altogether, but he was talked out of it by Barbara. "I don't want you to sit around the rest of your life thinking you *could have* made it to the majors," she told him. "We both know you're good enough to pitch in the big leagues, so let's stick it out a while longer and see what happens."

Larry talked to his coach the next day and gave him an ultimatum: "Either I get a chance to start within one week, or I plan to retire from baseball." Three days later he got his chance; he started a game against Austin and shut them out, in a brilliant two-hitter. He got another chance; he won again, and with that victory gained a spot in the starting rotation. In the next six weeks he pitched in nine games and racked up a phenomenal nine consecutive victories, including four shutouts. That got the attention of the Dodger front office. They needed a front-line starting pitcher, decided Larry Miller was outperforming every pitcher in their farm system, and called him up to the major leagues. It was an incredible turnaround. Six weeks after he had been on the verge of quitting, languishing on the bench of an AA farm team, Larry Miller was a starting pitcher for the Los Angeles Dodgers.

He played three years in the big leagues. During that 1964 season, he played alongside such all-time great pitchers as Sandy Koufax and Don Drysdale; and, though he never distinguished himself in their company, he was never embarrassed, either. He did a solid, workmanlike job—never a star, but always a reliable performer—that season for the Dodgers and the next two years for the New York Mets. After the 1966 season, he was traded to the San Francisco Giants, who sent him to their AAA team in Phoenix.

The next two years in Phoenix were Larry's last in professional baseball—and the most pleasant for him and his young family. "We loved Phoenix from the first day we rolled into town," he remembers. They bought a house in the suburban town of Scottsdale and settled into the life of the community to a degree they had never done in the many years of his career. When the Giants traded him again two years later, he simply said no. He retired after nine years of pro ball, finished a master's degree in civil engineering at Arizona State University, and went to work as a marketing consultant in the cement industry.

Larry's athletic career had a predictable impact on his family. Larry, Jr., became an outstanding high-school baseball player, also a pitcher. Kathy was involved in competitive swimming and track as early as her elementary-school days. Sports were always emphasized in the Miller household, and both youngsters responded by becoming exceptional athletes. Kathy was particularly good in distance events, as a junior-high runner. She won many ribbons, in such events as the half-mile run, the mile run, and the cross-country run.

On one occasion she ran in a citywide cross-country race, against seventy-five other junior-high athletes, and finished third. It was one of the first times her father had seen her run competitively, and he recalls his feelings that afternoon: "All the runners left the starting point—this great mass of kids—and they ran out of sight, because it was a cross-country race, not on a track. We waited for a long while, waiting for them to come back into view about two hundred yards from the finish line. Finally they came into sight, not a big mass of them any more, but just the first three runners. I'll never forget how it felt to see that little blonde girl bob up over the hill, running hard. I was so proud, I felt like crying."

It is an understandable emotion. Larry Miller is a

man who values the disciplines required for athletic achievement. One can imagine his pride in this plucky little daughter who showed him that she, too, knew how to run when it hurts—she, too, cared about competing and winning. He felt the pride of a father who sees his own best qualities mirrored in a child he loves.

Mixed with that pride were the enormous protective instincts that a father feels for his daughter. Larry came from the old-fashioned Midwestern tradition of the father as protector and provider. He is a strong, capable man, entrusted by parenthood with this fragile, pretty, thirteen-year-old girl, and all the powerful, primeval instincts of fatherhood rise inside him, making him want to care for her and see her safely to adulthood.

But now he was powerless to help her. She was his daughter and she was struggling for life and there was nothing he could do to help her. For Larry Miller, the night of the accident was a night of frustration and fear and helplessness.

And that first night outside the intensive-care unit at Scottsdale Memorial Hospital was also a night for memories. He remembered the last minute before Kathy had left the house that afternoon. She and her friend Sheri had been watching television in the family room, while Larry worked nearby. As they started out the door, he realized they had left the TV set on, and he yelled at Kathy to come back and turn it off. She did so, which delayed her departure by a few seconds. Over and over, those few seconds haunted Larry. If he hadn't called her back, he agonized, she would have been a few seconds farther along when the car passed by, and would have avoided being hit. It was an irrational thought, he knew, but it plagued him, nevertheless, and he played the awful consequences over and over in his mind that night.

There were other, better, memories. Kathy was an affectionate child; she and her father had always hugged and kissed each other unselfconsciously. That morning of the accident, she was late getting ready for school ("she was always late, always trying to sleep as long as she could") and made a quick rush into the kitchen to grab her sack lunch. Larry was sitting at the kitchen table. "She gave me a quick kiss good-bye. That morning, I gave her a hug, and I didn't let go of her right away. She tried to pull away from me, and said, 'C'mon, dad, let me go. I'm going to miss the bus.' I said 'Kathy, just give me a little extra time this morning. Dads need a little loving, too.' So she smiled and squeezed me, and for the next five or six seconds we just hugged each other, and then she ran out the door. Somehow I didn't want to turn her loose that day; I had an urge to hold her a little longer."

A premonition? Nothing of the sort. It was an ordinary exchange between a man and his daughter, and if she had not crossed Scottsdale Road just when she did, Larry Miller would not even have remembered it as being unusual. But she had crossed when she did. And the car had hit her. And now, assaulted by the realities and fears of the night, Larry Miller had nothing to do but wait and pray . . . and remember.

Chapter Five

KATHY made it through the night, and we regarded it as a victory. We had been told she might not survive that long; so, when the sun came up on Tuesday, we gave thanks and looked toward what Dr. Christensen had called the critical next twenty-four hours.

I felt so strongly during the night that God wanted me to look to Him for support that I prayed, early that morning, for Him to send to my mind Scriptures that I needed to hear. I have never been one to memorize Scripture. I should do more of it, I suppose, but memorization does not come easily to me, and I have never done much of it. That day, however, and throughout the weeks and months that followed, Scripture verses would just pop into my head. A verse of Scripture, or even just a fragment of a verse, would speak to me in my times of greatest crisis.

Scripture came to me that morning; Scripture that

speaks of physical healing. It was two verses that I
don't remember ever hearing until a few months before the accident, and they had even then been rather
difficult for me to understand. They were James 5:14,
15, verses that describe the biblical practice of anointing with oil. I found a Bible in the hospital and read it
carefully: "Is there any sick among you? Let him call
for the elders of the church: and let them pray over
him, anointing him with oil in the name of the Lord:
And the prayer of faith shall save the sick, and the
Lord shall raise him up. . . ."

I felt that God was talking to me through those verses, telling me what to do to help Kathy. The specific
activity of anointing with oil, however, was something
unknown to me. Larry and I had been members of the
Scottsdale United Methodist Church for many years,
but a few months earlier, a Baptist friend of ours,
Chuck Toon, had spent two hours telling us about
anointing, explaining the symbolism of the oil. Anointing the sick with oil did not mean that the oil itself was
magical in any way, he explained, but merely indicated
an individual's obedience to the command of Scripture. At the time he explained it, the entire idea
seemed purely an academic matter; we discussed it as
we might discuss any other interesting but irrelevant
topic. But now it became suddenly a Scripture with in-
tensely personal meaning for us.

My responsibility seemed clear: I was being led by
the Spirit of God to have Kathy anointed with oil and
prayed for. That evening, when the associate pastor of

our church came by the hospital, I laid the proposition squarely upon him. I quoted the Scripture to him, telling him that I felt God wanted this done and that we wanted him, as our minister, to do it, even though it is not generally practiced in the Methodist Church. He paused for a single, hesitating moment, then firmly replied, "Okay. Fine. If that's what you feel should be done, I'll do it. Just give me time to go home and get things together, and I'll be back to do it."

The next day I left the hospital to shower, change clothes, and try to get some rest. I had just stepped into the shower when the phone rang. It was a call from the hospital, telling me that our minister had arrived to pray for Kathy and to anoint her with oil. I quickly showered, jumped into my clothes, and headed back to the hospital. As I drove, it occurred to me that the verse in James 5 refers to the elders of the church praying for the sick. *Who are the elders of the church?* I wondered. Somehow I had never thought about that before, but I supposed that it must mean the other believers, other members of the body of Christ. I realized that I should have called someone else to join us in the anointing prayer, someone other than the minister, to represent the elders of the church. Immediately I thought of Chuck Toon, the Christian friend whose explanation of anointing had started this whole thing. *Why didn't I think to call him?* I berated myself. It would have meant so much for him to be with us when Kathy was anointed with oil.

I pulled into an empty parking place at the back of

the hospital, these thoughts flooding my mind, and stepped from the car just in time to see Chuck Toon pull into the parking spot next to me! That was the final confirmation that sealed it for me; I knew without a doubt, when I saw Chuck, that the Lord was directing the entire affair. This was Chuck's first visit to the hospital. I explained to him what was taking place, and we went upstairs together. There we met our minister and Larry and, joined by Dick and June Dennis, our close friends, we went into Kathy's room for prayer. We all held hands, to form a circle around her bed, anointed her with oil, and prayed for her healing. "We are surrounding Kathy with a circle of love," Dick said softly, after we prayed.

That very afternoon, barely half an hour later, we received word that Kathy was being transferred from the intensive-care unit to a private room. "We're moving her to five west," a nurse told us, and to me, five west sounded like the Promised Land itself! I accepted it as the confirming evidence that our prayers had been heard.

* * * *

Our spirits really lifted that afternoon. Medically, the prognosis for Kathy was still grim. She had shown no signs of regaining consciousness, and the doctors were telling us that the situation was still a critical, day-to-day thing. But spiritually, it seemed to Larry and me that the outlook was much brighter. She *had*, after all, survived the first night, then twenty-four hours, then forty-eight. She was hanging on. And all the time, I was getting a series of little assurances from the Lord that He was with us. There had been no big miracles, no spectacular visions, or anything of that nature, but as I went into room 516 to see Kathy, I counted all the small things I had to be thankful for, all the small signals I was receiving that things were going to be all right. I made a mental list:

First, there was the fact that Larry happened to be home when the accident occurred. On a typical day, he would not have been home; in fact, he would have been *driving home* on Scottsdale Road, past the intersection where the accident had occurred, just at the time that Kathy was lying on the highway.

Second, the site of the accident was only one and one-half miles from a fully equipped, expertly staffed fire station. They responded to the call in less than three minutes.

Third, one of the first persons to arrive at the scene of the accident was a physician—not only a physician, but one who was willing to stop immediately to offer aid.

Fourth, there was the way I was able to recall the phone numbers of everyone I needed to call when I arrived at the hospital.

Fifth, the appearance of Larry, Jr., at the hospital just as I prayed for help in reaching him seemed to me nothing short of miraculous.

Sixth, even Dr. Christensen's use of the word *guarded* spoke to me at a spiritual level. I understood that he used the word in a medical sense, to describe the critical nature of her injuries, but when he used the word *guarded*, I felt that the Lord was reminding me that Kathy's life was indeed guarded by God Himself.

Seventh, the unusual set of "coincidences" surrounding our anointing Kathy with oil, especially the almost immediate news that she was leaving the ICU.

Any of these, taken individually, might appear meaningless, but taken together, they all showed me an encouraging pattern. I ran over the string of events in my mind, and to me they all added up to evidence that the God who had been with me as I knelt on the highway on Monday was still with me on Wednesday night. I looked at the unopened eyes, the lifeless face of my little Kathy, and felt a strong, rising tide of faith build in my heart.

I was going to need it. Far more than I realized, in the days to come, I was going to need all the faith I could get.

Chapter Six

KATHY'S condition seemed to stabilize during the first few days after she was moved to five west. The immediate danger of death passed, and Dr. Christensen gave us cautiously optimistic reports of her progress. We began to expect her to gain consciousness at any time; we thought perhaps the ordeal was almost over.

Then, suddenly, the bottom dropped out.

It was Friday, the fifth day in the hospital. A nurse came into Kathy's room and asked me to sign papers that would authorize a brain scan. I thought it was a routine procedure and signed without giving it much thought. A few minutes later, Dr. Christensen came into the room, wearing his operating-room "greenies," with an unusually sober look on his face. He spoke tensely, tight-lipped: "I've got to find out why she's *going downhill.*"

Downhill! That word hit me like a sledgehammer. It

stunned me, almost like a physical blow. It was so negative, so jolting, I was staggered by it. *Downhill!* After all the prayers, all the hope, all the progress we thought she had made, the idea that she was getting worse was too much for me to handle. We had been sailing along on a cushion of unrealistic optimism, thinking Kathy would be awake and talking with us at almost any time, and now, suddenly, I could feel it all slipping away under the weight of that awful word *downhill.* The panic crowded in on me again, and I abruptly left the room.

I walked into the hallway, found a nearby waiting area, and started to pray. "Lord," I pleaded, "that word *downhill:* I just can't accept it as being from You, or that she's really going downhill." I felt the need to press for some kind of new assurance, and I prayed on: "Lord, if that word is not from You, please give me something to restore the peace I felt at the accident. I really do need some tangible sign that things are going to be AOK. I want something so clear that I can't mistake it." I used those very words and, finishing the prayer, I raised my head. At that precise moment, the double doors at the end of the hallway burst open, and through them walked Sharon Neff.

Sharon is a college girl who had once lived with us, and she was so close to the family, we called her our other daughter. She was a student at Northern Arizona University in Flagstaff, had heard about Kathy, and had driven down from Flagstaff to see us. She burst through those doors with a big smile on her face and practically shouted at me, "I'm here with a word from the Lord, to tell you that Kathy Miller is AOK!" The timing was so perfect and the connection between my prayer and her expression so close, that it could only have come from the hand of God. I claimed it as a direct answer from Him.

One of the remarkable things about that occasion was that such a positive, optimistic expression was totally out of character for Sharon. She would have more predictably come in crying and upset by the crisis at hand, full of expressions of concern at the seriousness of the problem. Anyone who knew Sharon well would have expected that of her; for her to throw the doors open and enter the scene with such a bright, buoyant message was too remarkable to dismiss lightly. I accepted her timely entrance as a gift to me, something given by God to offset the negative impact of the change in Kathy's condition.

By now it must be apparent that I had come to regard this entire crisis as a spiritual battle, with God on our side. Dr. Christensen has referred to this as my "religious strategy" for coping with the enormous stress that I faced, but I prefer to think of it in more simplistic terms. I simply believe that, as a child of God, I have the wonderful privilege of turning this kind of emergency into His hands and letting Him bear the load for me. As long as I seriously seek to do that, I believe He has promised to give me special strength and guidance. I didn't feel that this necessarily guaranteed that Kathy would live, or that she would ever regain consciousness, much less lead a normal life. What it did guarantee, I felt, was that whatever outcome occurred, we would be able to accept it—that we would all be at peace with it and be better off for having experienced it.

There was a time, only a few years earlier in my life, when I would have been completely unable to feel such an assurance from God: a time when, though I had been a Christian by the traditional definition, I was certainly a very different kind of Christian from what I am today. A change occurred in my life about nine years ago; a change that gave me a whole new outlook on God and my relationship with Him. About nine years ago, I experienced a new birth in Christ. I came to know Him in a personal, firsthand way.

Larry and I have always been what he calls "card-carrying Christians." We had grown up in the Methodist Church, in homes that emphasized Christian values and church attendance. (My great-grandfather was, in fact, a missionary to the Indians in the Old West.) My religious training was of the conventional type: Go to church on Sunday, say your prayers every night, and do good to your fellowman. But none of that had ever given me any real spiritual depth, and, looking back, I can see now that I never really knew who the person Jesus Christ was.

About nine years ago, I reached a point of great personal emptiness and dissatisfaction. Larry, Jr., was in school, and Kathy had just started day nursery. In a single summer, three of my closest friends moved away. I had more time on my hands than ever before, and I was lonely. I was searching for something deeper in life, though I didn't know that what I sought was necessarily spiritual.

One weekend, we visited friends in Albuquerque, who told us they had something important they wished to share with us. That night, in their living room, they explained their experience in the Holy Spirit. They were Baptists, and though they didn't regard themselves as charismatics, they described an experience with Christ that seemed to go even beyond that which we thought of as making someone a believing Christian. Our friend told us that he could be at the office and she at home, and they would feel the need of prayer together. They could feel each other's prayers, and they believed that the Holy Spirit was responsible for this unusual level of communication. I listened carefully, and that night, though I didn't say so, realized that God was trying to show me a deeper experience with Him.

The thing that held me back from seeking it was pride—plain and simple. I had spent my entire life, since I was a little kid, trying to be a "somebody"—and I resisted the idea of becoming some sort of holy roller. That sounds so crass, but that's the way it was. I had my concept of these superfervent Christians, and I was simply being a snob about the whole deal. That summer and fall, God led me to places where people above me on the social ladder were being used of the Spirit. He gradually showed me the pettiness of my pride and convicted me of it. In September of that year, I accompanied a friend to an interdenominational prayer meeting in a home in Scottsdale. There I prayed and asked Jesus Christ and the Holy Spirit to enter my life, and they wonderfully did. I had a tremendous sense of a new beginning with God—I was born again by the Holy Spirit, and I have not been the same since that day.

Sometimes I am asked if I am a charismatic, and I don't know how to answer that question. I know that God has come to live in my heart and has filled me with His Holy Spirit, and I have enjoyed many charismatic meetings, but I am not really interested in wearing any particular label to describe my experience. After that memorable day in September of 1971, I felt, through prayer, that I should stay involved in my local Methodist Church, and have done so. I had such a beautiful feeling, and I wanted to share it with as many people as possible, but I didn't want to do so in such an aggressive manner that people would be put off by it. In these past nine years, God has given me many opportunities to witness of His work in my life: in the Methodist Church, among Catholics and Protestants of all types, and in all sorts of personal encounters. That's good enough for me. I don't need to use a label to describe my experience with the Lord.

Since I was born again, I have felt many times that God communicates with me; He tells me things. I realize how hopelessly mystical that must sound to someone who is unaccustomed to such an idea, but I firmly believe that prayer can be a two-way street. God not only hears, but sometimes He also talks back, if we are willing to listen for His voice and willing to acknowledge that it is He who is speaking to us. I had to learn to slow down and give God a chance to take control of my life. I had been too busy, trying to schedule every minute of my time, trying to make life do what I wanted it to do. It took a real change for me to relax and let God take over my life, to relinquish things to Him and trust Him to work them out.

Along the way, I have found that if I let Him, He will tell me things. I call these little, personal messages from God my "inputs" from Him. They don't come as visions or voices or spectacular events, but rather as almost subliminal messages, as impressions, as a sense that God is showing me something He wants me to know.

Does that sound too way-out to believe? I suppose to many people it would, and I can understand that. My son teases me about my inputs from God; he calls me the "White Witch" whenever I start to talk about God showing me things. But it's true, nonetheless, and if I could understand it—well, then it wouldn't be so special, would it?

God's presence has never been more real to me—never in my life—than that day I knelt on Scottsdale Road and prayed for Kathy. God told me that everything was going to be all right, even if she died, somehow, it was going to be all right. Then, as I accepted that, He showed me that she was going to be more than she had ever been before. I didn't know how He intended to accomplish this, but I never doubted that Kathy was going to return, to be something more than she was before.

Anytime I heard a negative report or got discouraged, I would say, "Lord, if You want me to hang on to what You gave me at the scene of the accident, You need to send me something to restore that peace in me. Send me something or someone, or quicken my mind to a verse of Scripture. . . ." And He always did.

That's exactly what happened when Sharon's unexpected arrival coincided so beautifully with the doctor's report that things were going downhill. God knew I needed a word of encouragement, and He sent it to me through Sharon. That was the pattern. It was never easy, but it was always simple.

Chapter Seven

THE MILLERS were going to need all the encouragement they could get.

Kathy was indeed going downhill, and at an alarming rate. She was a critically injured child with a badly damaged brain, and the comfort that the Millers began to feel as she survived those first few days was medically ill-founded. Only the immediate threat of death had passed, and the medical staff at Scottsdale Memorial Hospital understood, much better than the Millers, that she was far from being out of the danger zone.

Dr. Fred Christensen is the young neurosurgeon who was on call the afternoon of March 14. Kathy became his patient. He is a small, compact man, with the brisk, tightly wound manner of a man who feels his time is extremely valuable—as indeed his is. According to his colleagues, he is a man of extraordinary professional skill; one Phoenix area colleague calls him "one of the very best neurosurgeons in the entire Southwest." He sees hundreds of brain-damaged patients, enough to eliminate from his mind any romantic notions of miraculous, sudden recovery. Kathy's case was a bad one, a very bad one, and Christensen feared that Barbara Miller might fail to understand just how great the odds were against Kathy ever recovering completely.

"Kathy had a bruised brain," he says. "The brain is inside a solid case—the skull. You bang it around, and it gets bruised. That bruised area swells, and it creates pressure on the brain. Much of Kathy's injury was to the brain stem, rather than the cortex. When the swelling in the brain goes down, the brain doesn't heal. It doesn't scar over and heal, like other areas of the body. If you ever kill a part of it, it's dead forever. Kathy had a severe contusion of the brain, and I thought she would probably have permanent brain damage. I thought she would never make a complete recovery. She might become ambulatory, maybe learn to dress herself and feed herself, but no more."

Christensen did not tell the parents that, of course—not in the first week. He simply told them to wait. "Wait and see," he said. "These things take time. We've simply got to give it time." There were, in fact, some very good signs, which indicated from the first week that Kathy had a good chance of making it. Her heartbeat was strong; her bowels were working; her pupils dilated briskly to light; by the fourth day, there was very little additional hemorrhaging in the brain.

But on March 19, the day that Barbara heard the upsetting news that Kathy was going downhill, her overall condition had taken a turn for the worse.

"We started getting in trouble," Christensen recalls. "Her temperature went up to 101 that day, and she began to deteriorate neurologically. The brain's need for oxygen goes up as the body temperature increases; and, since it was just getting by marginally, to begin with, it wasn't getting by at all, anymore. As that happened, she got worse. She became more stiff and rigid all over and less responsive. Over the next couple of days, we checked everything, to see if we could find the problem. We checked spinal fluid, lungs, urine, everything. We couldn't find infection anywhere. The problem was simply caused by the injury to the head: The brain wasn't regulating the temperature anymore."

Christensen and his staff were beginning a long, hard fight to "get ahead of all the medical problems" and to give Kathy a chance to get better. There was going to be no sudden, Hollywood-style awakening for her—of that they were certain. She had lapsed into a deep coma, and before she could emerge from it—if indeed she would—a long list of medical problems must be monitored and stabilized and eventually solved. As far as the brain was concerned, it was pretty much on its own, and very little could be done to speed its recovery. That was strictly a matter of waiting and, if one were so inclined, praying.

Christensen's job was to keep the patient healthy

enough otherwise to give the brain a fighting chance. "There's no way you can make the doctor some kind of hero," Christensen insists. "What is going to happen is going to happen, almost regardless of what we do. Nature is doing its thing. We simply do the best we can to help it along. If you get a positive outcome, it simply means you didn't make any mistakes. What kills these people is when you let something go wrong."

* * * *

In Kathy's case, there were other complications, caused by the broken leg she had suffered. The injury, pushed into the background by the more serious brain damage, now began to demand attention. Even if Kathy lived, even if she gained the power to walk, she might well emerge from the ordeal as a cripple, if the leg could not be effectively treated. That task belonged to Dr. Bryant, the orthopedic surgeon on duty at Scottsdale Memorial Hospital when the ambulance brought Kathy in. It was a case that would occupy him for many weeks.

"We took her to surgery immediately after she arrived at the hospital. She had a quite severe injury, a compound fracture of the right femur [thigh bone]. The bone was protruding through the skin, and there was a great amount of damage. Some of the muscle was ripped away. She lost lots of it; it was just gone. The bone from the upper leg was forced down, through the skin and into the back of the knee. You can lose a leg with that kind of injury, although it was never contemplated as an immediate procedure.

"We had to keep the wound open, to try to let it heal from the inside out. That's standard treatment with this kind of injury. We do that to try to prevent infection, but she developed an infection in the bone anyway, and we had to go back in, to take care of that. It was a bad break; we weren't able to set it immediately, and then, of course, she went into a coma, and that made the problem difficult to manage. When you have a brain injury, you get spasms in the muscles. In Kathy's case, this caused a realignment of the fracture, and that created more trouble."

It would be sixteen days after the original surgery before Bryant would be able to set the broken bone permanently. In the meantime, the leg had to be kept in traction, in order to keep the muscles from pulling the broken ends of the bone together in an undesirable fashion. It was a nasty complication, one which would create new problems in weeks to come.

* * * *

One week after she was hit, Kathy Miller lay unconscious in room number 516, her right leg suspended above the bed with its ugly wound still open, her broken leg unset, her breathing labored and slow, her body rigid and unresponsive, her fever out of control. She could no longer be regarded as a girl who was simply knocked out by a speeding automobile and who, having survived the blow, was now getting better. The picture was much darker than that. Kathy had sunk into a deep coma, and there were no guarantees that she would have any future at all.

Chapter Eight

COMA. That's a tough word. It has an ominous sound to it. It suggests a person who is barely more than a vegetable: alive, but permanently unresponsive, sunk in a stupor that no one fully understands. That word frightened Larry and me so much that we resisted using it for a while. But, after several days had gone by, we accepted the word and the idea. Whatever it meant, wherever it led, Kathy was in a coma.

She stayed in a coma day after day, and gradually we came to count in weeks, rather than days. The doctors battled a variety of medical problems as the weeks went by, but her comatose condition never changed. It was as if she had fallen into a deep sleep, from which she would never awaken. We settled into a routine after a few days: Larry and I would get up about 5:30 or 6:00 every morning, and one of us would call the hospital. We talked to the nurses' station on five west.

We always asked the same question: "Was there any change in Kathy last night?" And we always got the same answer: "No change." The nurses would always try to tell us something positive, such as, "She had a comfortable night," or "She seems to be doing well," but that always translated to the same message: No change.

After we called each morning, I fixed breakfast for Larry, Jr., at about 7 o'clock, and we would leave for the hospital. We were there by 7:30. We went straight up to the fifth floor to see Kathy, then went down to get a cup of coffee and wait for Dr. Christensen to come by on his rounds. We would always be there to meet him, always with a tiny glimmer of hope that he might give us good news of some sort. He was usually gone by 9:00, and soon afterwards, Larry would leave to go to work. I stayed at the hospital all day. Visitors would occasionally come and go. I would read or write letters, talk to Kathy (just as if she could hear me), and help the nurses take care of her. In the afternoon, Larry, Jr., would usually drop by after school for a while, and at dinner time the three of us would go out to get something to eat. We practically learned the Denny's Restaurant menu by heart. Larry and I would go back to the hospital until 9:30 or 10:00, then finally go home to bed.

Days wore on, and nothing seemed to change. The twenty-four-hour-a-day absorption in Kathy's condition put enormous stress on all of us, especially since there seemed to be no progress, nothing to be encouraged about, no hope that things would ever be any better.

The pressure began to show in our attitude toward Dr. Christensen. We knew him to be a good neurosurgeon, and were thankful that he was on the case; but, as weeks went by and there was no change in Kathy, we began to regard him as somewhat unfeeling. Larry and I would go to the hospital every morning with nothing but Kathy on our minds. We waited eagerly for Dr. Christensen to make his rounds, and every day we hoped for a change in her condition. But, when he arrived, he never lingered at her bedside. He usually stayed less than two minutes. He would force her eyelids open, look at her pupils, call her name a couple of times. Then he would scribble a few words on his chart, say something to the nurses, and away he would go. It all seemed so detached and clinical to me, so routine. I wanted so badly to hear him say that Kathy was getting better—and when he didn't, I grew impatient with him, as if he weren't trying hard enough or didn't care enough or *something!*

I was sensible enough to realize that my emotions were haywire on this point, and I wanted to avoid any negative feeling toward Dr. Christensen. So I did what I usually do in such a case: I made it a matter of prayer. "Show me something to help me understand this doctor," I prayed. And God showed me the analogy of Dr. Christensen as a relief pitcher on a baseball team.

When Larry was a relief pitcher, he would come into his team's game almost every night to pitch, always when the score was close and men were on base. In other words, he always pitched when the situation was bad, even critical. But, as a relief pitcher, he never got uptight or emotional about the situation. He knew he had to stay cool and detached, in order to meet the crisis. That was the comparison that God showed me. Fred Christensen always came into these cases when they were desperate, and he had to maintain the level of detachment necessary to make the right decisions and get the job done. I believe God helped me to understand this and to appreciate the degree to which Dr. Christensen was taking the only posture that was possible for a man with his responsibility.

As the coma continued, Kathy began to lose weight at an alarming rate. The hospital staff tried to stop the loss by increasing her caloric intake. They were feeding her through a tube down her throat, and would force down protein shakes, sometimes with melted butter and sugar in them, giving her as much as 5,000 calories a day, but still her weight went down and down. Her arms became little more than skin-covered bones; her breasts became totally flat. From a weight of 110 pounds before the accident, she dwindled to approximately 55 pounds. She came to look horrible, physically, but somehow God helped me not to dwell on that. Kathy had always been fastidious about her personal appearance, and I was determined to keep her looking as pretty as possible while she was unconscious.

I recall a photographer taking pictures at the scene of

the accident. The memory is merely a fragment, a small vignette; but I remember thinking, as I watched him point his camera at Kathy's twisted, bloody body, *Oh, please, don't take her picture in this shape. She would be embarrassed to be seen looking so bad!*

With Kathy lying unconscious, I felt the same way. I knew that Kathy, if she were awake, would want to be pretty, and it meant a lot to me to try to keep her looking good. When she was brought out of the ICU, there was so much blood in her hair that the nurses told me they would have to cut it. I was horrified. Imagine Kathy waking up to find all her hair gone! So I got a bottle of powerful, all-purpose cleaning liquid called LOC and rubbed each strand of hair with it. That girl had the cleanest hair in Scottsdale when I was through, and afterward, I shampooed her hair and blew it dry twice a week. I would change the style, putting it up in pigtails one time, curling it the next, and so on. That took lots of time, of course, and it was true that she was unconscious and would never know. But I was her mother, and I was glad she was alive at all, so to me it didn't seem so ridiculous.

After a couple of weeks, I got her out of hospital clothes. I went out and bought her some of those tube tops that the kids were wearing that spring, and they helped her look like a person again. A friend made brightly colored T-shirts, with matching ribbons for her hair. One day someone brought her a T-shirt that said I LOVE YOU on it, and the reaction of the nurses and hospital attendants who worked with her was amazing.

They walked in, saw that shirt, and broke into big smiles. They started responding to her as a person, not as an object. When a person is in a coma that long, it's easy to treat her like a piece of furniture, and I was determined we were going to keep relating to Kathy as a person, whether she knew what was happening or not.

I talked to her as though she could hear and understand everything I said. I would come into her room in the morning and say, "Hey, Kathy, good morning! What kind of night did you have? It's a beautiful morning outside. It's really pretty today. You're looking good, Kath. Just looking great!" I would tell her about things that were going on and read cards and letters to her. Sometimes people would come by the room and look at me as if I were nuts, but I really didn't care. It was not as if I were actually blocking out reality; I just wanted to stay in touch with Kathy as best I could, and this was my way of doing it.

We wanted Kathy's hospital room to be a positive environment. As a family, we had for years believed in the power of a positive mental attitude. We have been Amway distributors for several years, and that business experience introduced us to the ideas of such men as Norman Vincent Peale and Robert Schuller.

We really don't know how much Kathy could hear or what she was aware of when she was unconscious. Not even medical experts agree on that. But I believe that the subconscious mind was designed as a message center by God, just as He made every other part of the human body. We know that even when the conscious mind is not functioning, the subconscious mind continues to operate. So our conclusion regarding Kathy was this: Since we didn't *know* to what degree she might be aware of what was happening, we would be as positive as possible in her presence, even though she was in a coma.

We made a big point of this with the nurses, visitors who came to see us, the people who worked with Kathy or cleaned her room, and everyone else involved. We made a simple request: If you have something negative to say, please say it out in the hall. If a nurse had a negative report to give us about Kathy's condition, we heard it in the hall. We wanted nothing but positive talk, positive prayers, positive hopes in that room. We asked God to send people to visit us who would bring hope and faith, rather than having a stream of visitors with furrowed brows and eyes full of tears; and He did that. We wanted to keep fear and doubt out of that room. We asked friends not to console us or to feel sorry for us, but to join us in positive affirmation of God's work, which was going on in Kathy's body. We could not see it yet, but we believed it and we affirmed it daily.

In the same spirit, we hung posters on the walls that expressed positive ideas. I brought some of her stuffed animals fom home. Kathy's cheerleading-squad photo arrived one day, and we had it framed and hung it on the inside of the door. When people came, I showed it to them and said, "This is the girl you are working with. This is what she looks like. What you see lying in that bed is not the real Kathy Miller. Kathy is a beautiful, energetic, healthy girl; this is what she is going to look like again, when she gets better."

I brought cassette tapes of the New Testament and played them at her bedside, along with a taped speech called "The Atmosphere of Greatness" and other positive-thinking tapes. I taped religious music and some of her favorite popular music and let her listen to that—*her* music—because it was for her to hear, not me. And I do believe she was hearing and receiving those messages. To what degree, I don't know. But some of it was getting through. I also believe in communicating by touch, so I did that with Kathy. I gave her a facial two or three times a week. I rubbed lotion into her skin. I loved her through my hands, and I believe somehow it mattered.

I learned her every move. I was like a mother with a newborn baby; I could tell from the expression on her face when she was uncomfortable. I did things for her that may not have been done, otherwise. Compacted bowels, for instance, are a frequent problem with coma patients, so I fed Kathy pulverized bran tablets, and she never had a problem. I did these things on my own because I felt the Lord was leading me to do them. How long was I prepared to continue this way? I don't believe I ever thought of it. I didn't have any sense of time; time lost its importance to me at the end of the first week. That was a gift from God. I told the Lord, "Your time frame is mine, Lord. I give up counting. I'm not going to worry about days or weeks. It just doesn't matter, anymore."

Larry found it more difficult. He didn't find the peace, sitting in that room, that I found. He would come in, hold Kathy's hand, touch her, lean over and kiss her, whisper quietly in her ear, and leave the room, to pace the hall outside. He wanted to be near, but it was hard for him to stay right in the room. He was dealing with a different set of pressures. He had an entirely different type of stress to handle, and somehow he couldn't feel the peace I felt. I knew where he was, but I seemed unable to reach him with anything that would ease his burden.

Chapter Nine

LARRY had always been very protective of Kathy. Many fathers have special relationships with their daughters, and Larry and Kathy were particularly close.

Kathy was born when we were at Fort Sill, Oklahoma, during Larry's army days, in August of 1963. The most significant thing about that birth was the tenderness with which it was received by her dad. He had brought me to the hospital and returned home, at the orders of the army doctors, to wait. When the call came that a baby girl had arrived, Larry drove to the hospital and went first to the nursery, to see his daughter. Only then did he come to see me, and when he came into the room, he was crying. It was an unusually moving experience for him. He had wanted a daughter, and somehow it really touched him when he saw Kathy for the first time, and he cried.

She was a small baby (4 pounds, 11 ounces), born

prematurely by a full month. She was put immediately into an incubator, and in her first few days, lost ten ounces, as newborn babies often will. There was a regulation at the army hospital that babies born prematurely could not be sent home until they weighed at least five pounds, so I had to leave the hospital without her. Larry and I had to wait ten days for Kathy to reach the five-pound limit before we could have her. It was a long ten days. Every day we called the hospital to check her weight. It crept up an ounce or so each day, and finally they took her out of the incubator, bundled her up carefully, and let us take her home. It seemed as if the long wait made her arrival in our home even more exciting.

During the first few years of Kathy's life, Larry was still playing baseball, and we lived in many different cities. She and Larry, Jr., both developed a great sense of independence as a result, and Larry was proud of them for it. We spent one winter in the Dominican Republic, playing winter ball, and our Dominican neighbors gave Kathy a nickname. Betola, they called her. In their legendary history, Betola was a woman who, at all times, under all circumstances, could take care of herself. Kathy was only a toddler then, but she had a streak of stubborn independence. She would walk out of our yard to neighboring houses all by herself, knock on the door, and march right in. The Dominicans laughed and called her Betola. Larry was obviously pleased by the nickname; he took pride in his self-sufficient little preschooler.

As Kathy became older, she showed an interest in sports that further endeared her to her father. She came home from school one day and announced to him, "Dad, I'm on the swim team." He hadn't even known she was trying out, but she had joined a team that was organized through the local parks-and-recreation department. Later she made her junior-high-school track team in the same manner, qualifying for the team first, then announcing it to her father as an accomplished fact. We went to watch her run in several meets. She ran the mile, which can be a long distance for a preteenager. A mile is four times around a standard, 440-yard, oval track. When Larry saw Kathy run her first competitive mile, he was as excited as if she were running for an Olympic gold medal. It wasn't the fact that she won that pleased him—she didn't, in fact—but the way she fought and pushed those last two laps. "Look at her," he told me. "She's really working, now. Her body is wanting to quit; you can see it in her face. But she's reaching down there and gutting it out." And she was. Dogged determination showed on her face. She was highly competitive, and was always willing to push herself to win. Perhaps it was that determination that Larry admired the most.

Larry had only one daughter, and he was fond of saying that she was exactly what every father would like to see in a daughter. She was a cheerleader, a member of the Junior National Honor Society, and a good student, if not an exceptional one. What she lacked in raw IQ, she made up for with hard work.

Now it seemed to Larry that it was all gone, the golden carriage turned to a pumpkin, the dream became a nightmare. He had so many plans, so many ambitions for Kathy, and it seemed that with one crunching blow of that automobile fender, they were all destroyed. He remembers his state of mind during those long, painful weeks:

"I guess you'd have to say hope was really dead. I would sit by Kathy's bedside and see this skeleton of a little girl and try to visualize what she was like before—this effervescent, bubbly kid. My memory of her was fading, as if she would never exist again. My prayers were that she would be taken, rather than be stuck away in a nursing home, to vegetate as a nothing. I wanted her to be able to function as a normal kid. I would have gladly accepted less than perfect— but please, Lord, give me a reasonably normal kid. My hopes at that time were so modest; I couldn't allow myself to hope for more."

On the Saturday after Kathy was hit, Larry had been scheduled to escort an eighteen-year-old neighbor to the Scottsdale Honors Cotillion. The girl's father was deceased, and at this prestigious social ball, it is customary for the girls to be escorted and presented by their fathers. Her family had asked Larry to stand in as her father, and on the previous Saturday, he had taken her to the rehearsal and had rented his tuxedo. On Wednesday, the mother heard about Kathy's accident and called us, to offer Larry an out. He refused it. He would go anyway, he said, just as planned. That is the kind of courage Larry has. So that Saturday night, he dressed up in his tux and escorted Patty to the cotillion. It was a traumatic experience for him, surrounded all evening by freshly scrubbed teenage girls, all in their gowns, with that special adolescent glow—while his own Kathy struggled for life in a hospital bed a few miles away. That entire evening, he visualized himself escorting his own daughter to that honors ball, and the thought that it would never happen tormented him. He came home that night defeated, empty—and who could blame him?

Larry's problem was that he had always been able to control whatever situation he found himself in. He is a take-charge guy, a problem solver. He has always been strong and self-sufficient. And now, for the first time in his life, he had run into a problem that he absolutely could not solve. There was nothing he could do that would affect the outcome.

At one time, we were getting so much advice about what new hospital to take Kathy to and which new specialist to send for, that we both became very confused by it all. Larry, especially, was determined to do whatever it took to give Kathy the very best chance to survive. He would have incurred any debt or accepted any commitment, to provide for her the best possible care. But he didn't know whether to leave her where she was, at Scottsdale Hospital under Dr. Christensen's care, or try to move her to some other place out of state.

All this confusion in our minds peaked at about the fourth week. Larry asked a friend of ours, a medical doctor, about it. "Larry," the friend said, "I'm going to be honest with you. Kathy is in God's hands, now. There is no piece of equipment, no medical specialist, no other hospital that can do any more for her than is being done. You just need to stay where you are and wait it out. It's all in God's hands, now."

That was the reality that Larry had such difficulty accepting. Waiting—simply waiting—can be the toughest job of all.

While he waited, Larry had other pressures to deal with. Financial worries were at the top of the list. A serious, protracted hospitalization can be incredibly expensive. Larry had always provided a good living for us, but the kind of bills we were incurring now could bankrupt the average, middle-class family. Larry's first thought, after Kathy had gotten over the immediate crisis, was *How will I ever pay the bills*? He had hospitalization insurance, which would cover most of the cost, but even the remaining expenses added up to a staggering financial load. Our Amway business helped greatly; without it, in fact, we would have been financially swamped. It gave us an ongoing income that kept the wolf from the door, while we were in the worst part of the financial crisis. Without it, we might have lost our house or our automobile.

Apart from money worries themselves, Larry also had to contend with the pressures of his job. When the emergency struck, I could simply pick up and move to the hospital day and night, if necessary. For the first two weeks, Larry did the same. He called his boss to explain the situation, and his boss told him to take off as much time as he needed.

But on Thursday night of the second week, Larry got a call at about 10:00. It was his boss, telling him to come in to see him at 9:00 the next morning. We went to bed that night, and one of us said to the other, "I wonder what he wants," but we both knew what it would be. The next morning, Larry came back to the hospital after his meeting, took me downstairs to get coffee, and explained what had happened. He was almost bitter that morning: "Paul was very understanding of my situation, but his superiors insist that I get back on the job. Starting Monday, I've got to take vacation time, then time without pay." He was totally frustrated, so resentful that his company "can only see that the cement isn't being sold." He had no choice but to return to work, but it was a wrenching thing for him. From that time, he spent his days torn between the desire to be at the hospital and the demand that he stay on the job. It added more stress to an already difficult situation.

Through all this, I ached to share with Larry the special emotional comfort that I had received from God. I told him about my feelings and shared with him my inputs, but it didn't seem to speak to the pain in his own heart. Many nights he couldn't sleep. I would feel him slip from our bed and hear him walk down the darkened hall and stand at the door of Kathy's bedroom. He would just stand there and look inside, like a pilgrim at a shrine, and later, sometimes much later, he would slip back into bed beside me.

Larry was not reluctant to discuss his feelings with me, and many nights we would lie in the dark alongside each other and his anguish would pour out.

He recalls those bleak, sleepless nights: "Barbara seemed to have an inner peace about it that I didn't have. I was frustrated by it. I would have given anything to have that peace, but I just didn't. It kept me awake at night. In the daytime, I couldn't think of anything but Kathy. It dominated my whole life. I would be out in my car, going to a business appointment, and I would swing out of my way to drive by the hospital, just to look up at that window on the fifth floor and know that my little girl was in a coma in there, and it would almost kill me.

"I wanted to believe Barbara, when she told me things were going to work out, but how could I, when the doctors were saying *no*? She was always so calm and reassuring, but how could I listen to her? I thought she was being naive about the whole thing—that she was just ignoring reality. I was very concerned about how it might affect Barb if Kathy died and she had to realize all those inputs she was getting were wrong."

I often told Larry that I had relinquished Kathy to God's care, and he had to do that, too. "Quit trying to do it by yourself, Larry," I urged him. "You need to turn Kathy over to God."

Larry finally did that. He finally relinquished Kathy.

One night, he lay in bed with his back to me and sobbed like a baby. He cried longer and harder than he has ever cried in his life, and he prayed a prayer of relinquishment. Larry is a big man, a muscular, athletic man; but he has never been too big a man to cry. That night he finally was able to release Kathy to God, to trust God with the outcome. He never had the same inner peace that I had, but it was a turning point for him, and he slept better that night than he had in many weeks.

Chapter Ten

SOMETHING about the Kathy Miller case affected people in an unusual way.

Individuals who crossed the Millers' path during those months were drawn into their orbit, perhaps attracted by the story of this pretty, young teenager fighting such a staggering array of medical and neurological problems. There was something about the Miller family that inspired a great many people, and interest in Kathy's progress became widespread around Scottsdale.

Dr. Jack Jewell, for example, did not simply disappear from the story after he stopped on the highway to administer aid that day. He went home from the scene, but couldn't get the girl off his mind. He called the hospital later that night to ask if she had survived, and the next morning, he stopped by the intensive-care unit at Scottsdale Memorial to see her. When she was moved to a private room later in the week, he began going by to see her almost every day.

"When I met the family," Jewell recalls, "we became friends very quickly. They were holding out so much hope. I just kept saying, 'Well, let's pray for the best.' I knew it was possible she would come out of the coma and be a vegetable. I learned a long time ago to be careful what you pray; you may get an answer! I would tell them, 'If she's going to be all right, maybe one of these days she'll open her eyes and be all right. And if she isn't, then maybe one of these days she'll sleep away.'

"They were always such believers that one day she would be one-hundred percent okay. That rarely happens, you know. As an outsider looking in, my medical judgment was getting rather dark, as the weeks went on. It was interesting to observe their faith and determination as a family. But I felt that the hopes were getting rather dark. There is no question that, in those first few days, the medical expertise of Fred Christensen and his staff kept the child alive. They got her over some pretty rough times in those first fifteen days. After they got her over the acute problems, it was a waiting game."

*   *   *   *

Another character in the drama of March 14 who was drawn into that waiting game was Tim Hoffman, the paramedic with the Scottsdale fire department who treated Kathy at the scene. Unknown to the Millers, Hoffman's decision to ride in the ambulance to the hospital with Kathy was not an easy one. He made the trip in violation of regulations and in direct disobedience of his superior's orders. It was one of those spur-of-the-moment decisions made on principle, and in so acting, he ran the risk of losing his job. There was a specific fire department regulation—since modified—stating that the engineer of a fire truck must not leave his vehicle, for any reason, at the scene of a call. As Kathy was loaded into the ambulance, however, Hoffman felt she needed to be attended. He feared she would not reach the hospital without a collapse of her blood pressure and heartbeat, and knew he needed to be with her, if that should happen.

He stepped over to his captain as Kathy was taken to the ambulance. "Somebody's got to go with her in that ambulance," he said. There was no answer.

"There's just no way around it, captain. Someone's got to go, and I'm going."

"You can't go," his captain replied. "You know the rules."

A man named Herb Drinkwater, a member of the Scottsdale city council and a friend of Hoffman's, was standing with them. Hoffman looked at Drinkwater and said it again: "Somebody's got to go!"

"It's up to your captain," Drinkwater replied.

Hoffman looked back at the captain. Time was racing past. The captain wouldn't budge. "You can't go, Tim," he repeated flatly.

That did it. "Well, I'm going," Hoffman said simply, "and I'll just pay the consequences later." And with that, he climbed into the back of the ambulance, closed the heavy rear door, and signaled the driver to depart.

When Kathy had been safely delivered to the hospital, Hoffman had time to think about what he had done. He decided to call his battalion chief immediately, to try to explain why he had done what he had done. (The battalion chief is the head of emergency units in the entire Scottsdale area.) By the time Hoffmann dialed the number, Hoffman's captain had already called the chief, to report Hoffman's violation of procedure. Within five minutes, the chief himself walked through the doors of the hospital. He walked up to Hoffman, who was braced for the worst.

"Are you ready to go back to work?" the chief asked quietly. It was not what Hoffman had expected.

"Do I still have a job?"

The chief grinned. "Yeah, you sure do," he answered. "Come on, I came to give you a ride back to the station."

They walked outside, toward the chief's car. "If you're wondering why you're not in trouble," the chief grunted finally, "I'll tell you. If it had been my daughter out there, I would have wanted you to do just what you did. Enough said?"

Hoffman nodded. "Enough said."

The next day, Tim Hoffman, like Dr. Jack Jewell, called Scottsdale Memorial Hospital, to inquire about the girl in the accident. A few days later he found his way to her room and met her parents. After that, he was a frequent visitor. "I've been on thousands of calls and seen thousands of accident victims, but I've never—ever—gone to see one of them afterward. Once I get them help, I forget about them, and I'm on my way. But there was something about her that sort of drew me to go and see her," Hoffman explains. "I went to the hospital a lot after that, every day I was off duty, for a long time. I guess I really got involved, and I don't have any regrets at all. I don't have any specific religious beliefs, but, after seeing what happened with Kathy, I think that would make anybody a believer in something."

Other people not directly involved in the accident reached out to help the Millers. Members of the Scottsdale United Methodist Church rallied to their support, and there were reports of many other congregations in the area offering special prayer for Kathy. Business associates in the Millers' Amway organization were particularly quick to lend a helping hand. Along with members of the Millers' church, they organized a rotating schedule of families to cook dinner each night and deliver it to the Miller home, ending the need for those monotonous restaurant meals. One day the Millers received a call from a wealthy Amway friend in another state, who told them he would send a blank check to them, to help with their medical expenses. "You have not because you ask not," he told them, "and I want you to know that my checkbook is your checkbook."

Other people supported the family simply by their prayers and expressions of support. The Millers received letters and cards from people whom they had never met, pledging their prayers. One night, Barbara and Larry were staying all night at the hospital and were asleep on a waiting-room couch. Barbara could sense someone standing over her, and opened her eyes. It was one of their business associates, one who also was a believing Christian. "Don't be startled," he whispered to her. "I'm working swing shift tonight at my job. I'm between shifts, and God told me to come down here and say a few prayers over you two. Please go back to sleep; I didn't mean to wake you." Barbara closed her eyes and dozed off again, and when she woke up, the friend was gone.

That kind of support was responsible, at least to some degree, for the seemingly inexhaustible hope that the Millers maintained. They had an incurable optimism, which both attracted and inspired a wide range of individuals who moved into their lives during this time. But the real issue was not Larry and Barbara's attitude, but whether or not Kathy would ever wake up again. All the concern of a Jack Jewell or the heroism of a Tim Hoffman or the love and support of a million friends would not affect that outcome one iota. The big question was still very much unanswered: Would Kathy Miller ever wake up? And if so, when? And in what condition?

Chapter Eleven

DR. BRYANT told us he was proceeding with the treatment of Kathy's leg as if she would someday use it again.

A few weeks after the accident, Kathy was again taken into surgery. It seems rather ironic that a patient already in a coma would require anesthesia, but that was the case. The doctors pulled her leg into the proper position, set the bone, and put her in a body cast that stretched from foot to hip on the right side and encircled her waist. Only her toes stuck out. That large cast was necessary because it was important to immobilize her leg as much as possible. Comatose patients do a lot of random thrashing about in bed, in involuntary, reflexive movement. In Kathy's case, the nasty, compound fracture simply could not take that kind of abuse, and it was necessary to keep her in a cast that would prevent her from causing further damage to the leg.

The cast caused problems. It was a situation in which the leg injury complicated the brain injury, and vice versa. Each made it more difficult to treat the other.

Kathy's condition worsened almost immediately after surgery on her leg. Her temperature started to climb again on April 1, and the hospital staff seemed unable to control it. She was also obviously very uncomfortable. She would moan and move restlessly in her bed. Something was wrong with her. Her coloring was bad, and she had dark, ugly circles under her eyes. The doctors and nurses kept trying to find the problem, but were unsuccessful, and it was becoming a matter of great concern.

It was Palm Sunday—April 3. Kathy had been in the cast only three days at that time. Just before church that morning, I received a call from a friend of mine, a Baptist minister in California. He explained his reason for calling: "I've really been feeling your spirit this morning, Barbara, and I have a message from the Lord for you and Larry. I feel that God has given me a verse of Scripture for you." And with that, he read Psalms 27:13, 14. It was meant especially for us, he said, and he had felt so led by God that he was calling from the West Coast to tell us so. "I had fainted, unless I had believed to see the goodness of the Lord in the land of the living. Wait on the Lord: be of good courage, and he shall strengthen thine heart: wait, I say, on the Lord."

I almost cried out with joy, when he read that verse.

One phrase in verse 13 was the key for me: ". . . in the land of the living." I had been trying to prepare myself for whatever came—even Kathy's death—and this verse seemed to be telling me that I need not make that sacrifice. He was going to show His goodness in *the land of the living!* That was the cushion God gave me to go to the hospital on that day. Kathy was going to live! It seemed a direct promise from God Himself.

When we got to the hospital after church that afternoon, Kathy looked horrible. Her stomach was pumped up like a toad's. Her tummy, which had been loose in the body cast two days earlier, now pushed tightly against it, even bulging over the top. Dr. Christensen came in to check on her, and when he tapped on her stomach, the sound was like tapping on a ripe watermelon. Suddenly it became apparent that there was a blockage of some sort; somehow, all those liquids that were being forced down the tube into her stomach were not being passed on through to the intestines. Dr. Christensen ordered abdominal X rays, and they confirmed the hunch: Gastric retention, he called it. The new body cast was pinching off a nerve that controlled the passage of matter from the stomach to the intestines. The nurses brought in a stomach pump and, within three hours, had pumped a gallon and a half of vile-looking fluid from her stomach. With that, Kathy seemed to relax and rest more comfortably, and her temperature began to go down again.

Looking back at it, that Palm Sunday incident was only one of a series of small emergencies that came and went during Kathy's ordeal, and perhaps it was not a very memorable one to anyone other than Larry and me. To us, at that time, however, it was a major victory. It seemed that just as things were beginning to slide downhill again, God sent an encouraging word of Scripture, then backed it up by giving us a small victory in Kathy's medical situation. As if to remind me of that, God sent another beautiful Christian friend to visit us that same afternoon. It was late in the day, and Larry and I were taking a short nap, lying on the waiting-room couches. The man said he had come by to read the Bible to Kathy, because the Lord had impressed him to do so. He knelt by her bedside, opened his Bible, and began to read. I could hardly believe my ears! The passage was Psalms 27, and when he got to verse 13, ". . . *the goodness of the Lord in the land of the living,*" there was no doubt that God had sent him there, to seal our faith in His continuing watch and care.

* * * *

The body cast continued to complicate Kathy's medical problems, and a couple of weeks later, it precipitated a situation that very nearly pulled the rug out from under me, emotionally.

It was about the middle of April, and Kathy was once again fighting a high body temperature. The reason correct body temperature is so crucial to the recovery of a brain-damaged patient is that the brain—even an uninjured brain—cannot function properly when body temperature is excessively high. An injured brain is struggling to operate; the patient is virtually fighting to regain enough neurological function to come out of the coma. Even slightly elevated body temperatures can make that vital difference between a brain that is recovering from injury and one that is not. The problem is compounded by the fact that it is the brain itself which regulates body temperature. So the struggle to combat fever is one of the major concerns of a doctor treating a comatose patient.

Naturally, an infection anywhere in the body can raise the patient's temperature dangerously, putting the recovery of the patient in serious jeopardy.

When Kathy's temperature began climbing again, about the middle of April, we were worried. I began to pray a great deal about it, since no one could figure out why it was happening. The hospital staff did various blood studies and other tests, but could find no infection. I was at the hospital one night during this time, when I noticed a small, reddish patch of skin at the base of Kathy's cast. We looked underneath the edge of the cast and immediately saw the source of the problem. There was a large, ugly sore, about four inches in circumference, at the base of the spine, under the cast. As Kathy had lost so much weight, her body had begun to slip and slide under the cast. The sore had eaten down into her flesh, forming a deep, infected hole, as if her flesh had been carved away with an ice-cream scoop. The area around the sore was red and inflamed. It was obviously the infected spot that was causing Kathy's temperature problems.

I was repulsed by the sight of the sore but delighted that we had found the problem. This was something that could be fixed—the sooner the better—by cutting away the cast, to get air down into the infected area and allow it to heal. I practically ran to the phone, to call the orthopedic surgeon. Instead of Dr. Bryant, I reached one of his partners. I explained the situation to him and asked if he could come down to the hospital and fix the cast. He responded with an abrupt refusal. "Look, Mrs. Miller," he snapped, "I'm not coming down there tonight, just to take care of a bedsore. A bedsore is nothing. If you want something to worry about, why don't you worry about whether she ever wakes up or not? Worry about whether she'll ever have a mind or not. Why don't you quit bothering me about a little thing like a bedsore and spend your time worrying about something important?"

It was an unbelievably cruel outburst. I had the composure to terminate the conversation coolly and unemotionally, but after hanging up, I almost immediately dissolved into tears. I had to pray over it half the night, to keep from being too upset to sleep. That was, perhaps the lowest point, emotionally, that I had reached. I had been trying so hard to keep my mind off the negative possibilities, which he so graphically described to me on the phone. His recital of them was a blow I was barely able to handle.

The next morning, Dr. Christensen cut the cast away from the infected area. After the problem was taken care of, I called Dr. Bryant and explained the incident of the night before. I was determined to be unemotional about it and to display a Christian attitude, and I think I did so. As I recall, "abrasive" was the strongest word I used to describe his partner. Later that day, to his credit, the partner called to apologize. I told him he was forgiven. "Just be thankful, though, that I had the spiritual resources to handle it," I added. "The next time, it could be a parent who is hanging on to hope by a slender thread, and your attitude could do him in."

* * * *

Life was lived on the ups and down of Kathy's daily condition through the month of April and into May. Sometimes it was a roller coaster: good news today, bad news tomorrow; temperature up today, down tomorrow; first a week of hopeful signs, then a week of nothing. Sometimes we felt that we were fooling ourselves, to think it would ever be different. After two months, Dr. Christensen noted that Kathy "wasn't terribly improved." Kathy was still "just staying ahead of the game," he felt. It seemed at times that we were merely making it from one small crisis to the next, never getting nearer to the day when she would come back to us, when she would open her eyes and see us and know us again.

We realized that time had become our enemy. The longer she stayed in that coma, the less her chances of being normal, if she woke up. She wasn't making any forward movement, and we had to entertain the possibility that she might *never* come out of it. We tried not to put a time limit on it. We were just looking for that one, little breakthrough. Sometimes one eye would twitch open for a second, and Larry would go to her and pry the other eye open. He would wave his hand in front of her face while he held her eyelid open, trying to get a response. He was just clinging to a hope that some flicker of life would show. Many times he would try to talk to her. "Wake up, Kathy," he would beg. "Please, just wake up for Daddy." It was as if he knew Kathy was down in there somewhere, and he was trying desperately to get through to her. Nothing ever worked, of course, and he never really expected it to. We both knew that it was a thing that could not be forced.

But all along, interwoven with the question marks, were the encouragements, the inputs from God, the emotional lifts that kept us going. Often it was a little thing. One afternoon, when Kathy was starting to look so emaciated, we were outside at home, doing yard work. Larry looked over at a little shrub and remembered that one year earlier, that bush had almost died. It had withered down to a stalk and a couple of small shoots. Larry had been ready to dig it up and replace it. Instead, for some reason, he decided to try to save it. He fertilized it, pruned it, weeded around it, watered it, took care of it—and now it was a big, healthy shrub. We looked at that shrub that afternoon and took heart from it. It was so like Kathy! We felt it was another way God was talking to us, telling us not to give up on Kathy.

Near the middle of May, Kathy's class of eighth graders graduated from Cocopah elementary school. She was to graduate with honors, and we went to receive her diploma. It was a very emotional experience for both of us. We sat and watched those 300 kids parade by in the graduation ceremony, all of them healthy and vibrant, smiling and enjoying themselves—and we thought of our Kathy, lying in a coma across town. We found ourselves following the alphabetical order of graduates, and when her time would have come, we tried to visualize her, marching forward.

When all the other diplomas were given out, the principal announced: "Now, accepting for Kathryn Suzanne Miller, her parents." As we walked up, all those 300 kids, then all their parents in the audience, jumped to their feet and applauded. We stood there and cried like two big babies. We suddenly realized that all these people *did* know about Kathy, and they were standing with us in our struggle. We were not alone. There was a great, loving God with us, and there were all these people who cared; and just knowing that, made the load a lighter one.

Chapter Twelve

WHEN THINGS began to happen, they happened quickly. After two months of little progress, as one of the doctors described it, "Things started to change, all of a sudden."

The Millers were so absorbed in Kathy's condition they had virtually memorized her every move, and they began to detect small, positive signs at about the ninth week of her coma. The Millers had been constantly warned by the hospital staff not to interpret Kathy's random, reflexive movements, as a positive sign. She had been moving about in this fashion for several weeks: spontaneous, flailing movements of the right arm, a flicking motion with one of the fingers of her right hand (which usually was balled into a fist), rolling her head from side to side, and occasional moaning.

All these behaviors are typical of the long-term

comatose patient, and do not necessarily indicate that the patient is beginning to come out of the coma. Larry and Barbara had learned this, and no longer took hope from these random movements. By early May, Dr. Christensen felt the time had come to try to communicate with Kathy in some way. "What we do about this time," he explained, "is see if we can somehow get through to them. We might ask them to open their eyes, lift a finger, or follow simple commands." Kathy could do none of this. There was still no communication.

In the ninth week, though, the Millers received a hint that the breakthrough might be approaching. It came from an unlikely situation: a simple refusal to swallow a foul tasting bit of food. Barbara is something of a health-food enthusiast, with a long-time interest in nutrition. Kathy's dramatic loss of weight and her general physical deterioration greatly concerned her mother, who, in her predictable take-charge style, set out to do something about it. She acquired a mortar and pestle and pulverized her favorite nutritional supplement—a vitamin-loaded tablet called Nutrilite Double-X—into a powdery mixture. She added to this substance liberal amounts of prune juice. Having produced a large batch of this homemade concoction, she set out for the hospital, to solve Kathy's nutritional deficiencies. It was rather typical of her practical, problem-solving approach.

Kathy was at this time swallowing liquefied foods. She was no longer being fed through a tube down her

Father-and-Son Day at Shea Stadium, when Larry was with the Mets. Larry, Larry Don, Kathy, Barbara.

Kathy in her elementary-school cheerleader's uniform, before the accident. *Below*: A favorite photo, made just within minutes of the twenty-four-hour period prior to the accident. Helping plant the family garden. Within each twenty-four-hour period, only God can know the total events.

Home again! A shell of the
girl she had been, but, thank
God, *at least* a shell.

Our doctors advised us to wait until later for pool activities, but we felt the water was a benefit, so we prayed and put her in the pool. *Below*: Day number two at home. Kathy attempts her first smile on command.

Friends have been very meaningful. Here a few close friends encourage Kathy and help her move toward communication. *Below:* Kathy working out on the bicycle with Scott Clark, her therapist, August 1977.

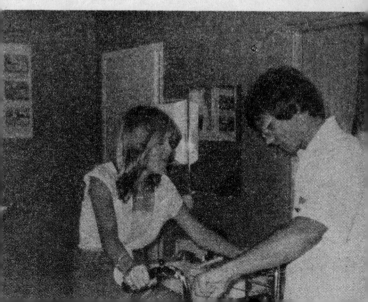

Larry and Kathy in October 1977. Notice that her eyes are still "not right." *Below*: Receiving her trophy from Dr. Art Mollen for Most Courageous Runner in North Bank's 10,000-meter run, November 1977.

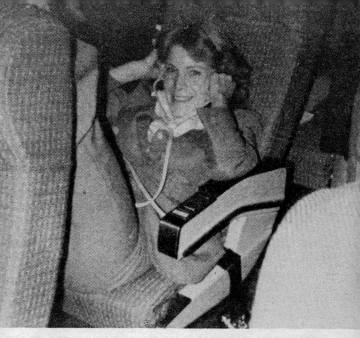

Kathy on the flight to London, February 1978.

Kathy and Larry Don walking along the River Thames in Hyde Park, London, February 1978.

Kathy makes a snowball at the Belfast Airport, February 12, 1978. This was the first snow she remembered. (Sport and General Press Agency photo.) *Below:* Kathy running with Mary Peters, pentathlon champion of the 1976 Olympics, at her track in Belfast, Ireland, February 12, 1978. (All-Sport photo.)

Her first opportunity to try on her International Award for Valour in Sport, February 15, 1978. (Sport and General Press Agency photo.) *Below:* On the Mike Douglas Show after returning from the award ceremonies. (Michael Leshnov photo.)

Her recovery required a lot of work and love. (Brian Payne photo.)
Below: Running was both therapy and fun. (Stephen Kelley photo.)

Kathy with paramedic Tim Hoffman (left) and his superior, March 1978. *Below:* Homecoming princess, November 1978.

Barbara and Kathy share a quiet moment together. (Jeffery R. Werner photo.) *Below:* Kathy and Larry at the opening night of the Dodgers' 1979 season. Kathy threw out the first ball of the season for the Dodgers. (Photos courtesy of Los Angeles Dodgers, Inc.)

Barbara, Steve Garvey, and Kathy at Dodger opening-night ceremonies, April 1979. *Left:* "Springing" has been a major part of Kathy's rehabilitation to facilitate speech and motor coordination. (Mick Paladin photo.)

What a joy, to return to the active life she once led. (Jeffery R. Werner photos.)

Kathy with Rosalynn Carter. Kathy was invited to the White House on her way home from the award ceremony in 1978. *Below*: Larry Don, Barbara, Kathy, and Larry Miller. (Jeffery R. Werner photo.)

The award presented to Kathy for her inspiration to handicapped children in Arizona. (Jeffery R. Werner photo.)

throat, but with a syringe, and was now spontaneously swallowing anything squeezed into her mouth. She was being fed, in this manner, on a diet of baby foods and protein shakes. Barbara asked Dr. Christensen if she could feed Kathy her prune juice and vitamin mixture; he, remarking that he knew of no way it could hurt Kathy, gave her permission to do so. For several days, Kathy was fed the mixture, swallowing reflexively each time it was squeezed into her mouth. But one day in that ninth week, Kathy did something she had never done before: She accepted a mouthful of the mixture, then, rather than swallowing it, she spit it all out—all over her chin and face. Barbara tried again; once again, Kathy stubbornly spit the mixture out.

"Did you see that?" Barbara asked her husband. "She just spits it all out; she won't swallow it. I wonder what would cause her to do a thing like that?"

Larry laughed. The answer was obvious to him. "Have you ever tasted that stuff?" he asked. Barbara had never bothered to do that, so she tasted it and found it to be more vile tasting than she had imagined! "Of course, Kathy spit it out," she explained. "This stuff tastes horrible! I wouldn't eat it, either!"

And so the Millers laughed about Barbara's nutritional invention, but behind the laughter there was a note of growing hope, a hint of change for the better. They had been falsely optimistic before, and had been disappointed before, so they knew the folly of overinterpreting any small incident. But, at the same time, it *was* a new, positive sign. It was a clear example of

Kathy responding to her environment in a way she had not done before. She had been passively, mechanically swallowing that awful-tasting mixture, and now she refused it. She spit it out. She *knew* it tasted bad, and she spit it out! Maybe, the Millers hoped, there was finally a bit of light at the end of the tunnel.

After that, Kathy would frequently spit things out that didn't suit her. She was still deeply comatose, and this was the first type of purposeful activity in which she engaged. The Millers recall another incident that week that indicated the rising level of their expectations for her. Larry was feeding Kathy one afternoon, and during the feeding, she constantly spit the food out. He would squeeze it into her mouth with a syringe, and she would immediately push it back out with her tongue. He tasted it; it tasted okay. He squeezed in another mouthful; she pushed it out again. This time, determined to get the job done, he spoke to her sharply. "Look, Kathy, you're *going* to eat this! You need it, and you're going to eat it, so just go ahead and swallow!" And as he said it, he slapped her. Not hard—he just cuffed her a bit—but it was more than a playful smack.

Reflecting on that incident, later in the day, Larry and Barbara realized that it showed a new, positive attitude on Larry's part. He was behaving as a normal father to a normal child, not as a grieving father to a dying cripple. Contrast that exchange between Larry and Kathy with earlier ones, times when he would beg her, "Kathy, if you'll just wake up, I'll give you anything you want, honey." Those were pitiful, desperate expressions. Smacking her, as he had done, represented progress from that earlier style. It showed that Larry had a growing expectation that she would recover. It was the gradual progress from "Please don't die, Kathy," to "Eat this stuff, so you'll get better faster." Emotionally, the distance from the first attitude to the latter one is a long, tough road to travel, and Larry was obviously getting there.

The stage was set for a breakthrough.

Chapter Thirteen

WE FELT SO strongly that Kathy was near the end of her coma that we hated to leave the hospital each evening. Every day was a day of expectation. We always got up in the morning saying, "Today's going to be the day!" We would hype ourselves up during breakfast and on the way to the hospital: "Today's the day Kathy's going to do something!"

When she first went into a coma, we had some sort of Hollywood, late-show idea of how she would finally come out of it. We had an image of her, lying peacefully asleep for a few days, then suddenly one day waking up, brushing her hair aside with her hand, and saying something like, "Oh, my, where am I?" or "What day is it?" or "Would somebody please bring me something to eat?"

We learned it doesn't work that way. A brain-damaged patient doesn't usually "wake up" from a

coma; he struggles and fights his way out of it, a little
at a time. There are no romantic, Hollywood-style
scenes, in which the victim is comatose one hour and
completely lucid the next. The process is much more
gradual, much more awkward and painful, than that.
But there definitely *is* a time when the patient comes
out of the coma; there is that first time she acknowl-
edges some message from the outside world and signals that she is there and can hear and understand
what is said to her. We were now confident such a
time was coming for Kathy, and how eagerly we
looked forward to it!

When it came, Larry was there to enjoy it. That is
the way I wanted it to be. I felt that God had been
communicating with me on a spiritual level all along,
and it was those spiritual inputs that I needed. Larry,
on the other hand, with his engineering background
and temperament, was a great deal more practical
about things, and he needed tangible, clear-cut
evidence—the outward and visible signs from God. I
believe God let him be the one to see those firsts in
Kathy's development for that reason, and I was delighted. God gives each of us exactly the kind of support we need, when we need it.

It was the last week of May. Kathy was in her tenth
week of unconsciousness. Larry came by the hospital
one afternoon, to stay in her room while I left to run
some errands. The nurses came in to change the sheets
on Kathy's bed. Their procedure in doing this was to
lift her out of her bed, sit her up in a chair, tie her to

the chair with a bed sheet to keep her from falling off, then change the linens and put her back into bed. Larry helped them move her; and, as they placed her in the chair, she moaned and rolled her head, as if she were uncomfortable. One of the nurses stuck a pillow behind her back, and, offhandedly, talking more to herself than to Kathy, the nurse said, "There you go, Kathy. Is that more comfortable?" She certainly was not expecting an answer; she was merely talking aloud, in the way one does around a coma patient.

But, when the nurse asked the question, Kathy nodded! It was a slight nod, barely a nod at all, but it was clearly a nod in response to the question. Larry saw it, and he looked excitedly at the two nurses. "Did you see that?" he shouted. Both nurses had seen it. The three of them stood, stunned. They were afraid they might have imagined it. Larry asked the question again. Kathy's eyes were still closed; she looked no different, but again she nodded. Her head barely moved, maybe an inch up and down, but this time there was no doubt. There could be no mistake; they had spoken to Kathy Miller, and she had answered!

It was a big moment—the moment we had awaited for so long—and the excitement spread through five west in a flash. The nurses could hardly wait to get outside the room, to tell the other nurses and attendants on the floor. By the time I returned to the hospital, almost everyone on five west had heard the news, and Larry was waiting impatiently to tell me all about it. It was an extremely emotional experience for us.

And the activity didn't stop right away. Several times throughout the rest of the afternoon, Kathy made small gestures that indicated a level of awareness we had not seen before.

Larry put her in a wheelchair, tied her to the chair, so she could sit in a slumped, semi-erect position, and rolled her downstairs. It was something we had never dared try previously. He pushed her outside, onto a quiet, sun-drenched patio area. It was one of our fabulous, Arizona late-spring days, and he wanted to savor it all with his daughter. He wanted to sit in the sun with her, to let her feel its rays warm her body, to introduce her to the feelings of life again. Larry had a cup of iced soda in his hand, drinking it as they sat silently in the sun together. He decided to try to feed some of it to her; he put his hand under her chin, tilted her head back gently, and let a bit of the soda trickle down her throat. Her eyes were still closed, but she swallowed. Larry stepped back and looked at her. Slowly, ever so slightly, Kathy nodded again, just as she had in the hospital room. She wanted more soda! It was an exhilarating afternoon, and Larry and I were so excited by bedtime that we could hardly sleep.

The next morning, Kathy showed no response to any specific communication from us. Even so, she seemed generally able to register more feeling. Larry tickled her—something she had enjoyed as a younger child—and she flinched and moaned as he did so.

When Dr. Christensen made his rounds, he had already heard the news of Kathy's nodding. His reaction was cautious, but it was cautiously optimistic. He agreed that this was a very good sign, but warned us against leaping too quickly to the conclusion that Kathy would now emerge completely from the coma. He was in a difficult spot, when one looks at it from his perspective. He was anxious that we not build ourselves up for a big disappointment, and he worked hard to keep us from expecting too much from Kathy too fast. At the same time, he was also emotionally involved in her case, just as we were. He was, in his own professional way, as happy to see the new development as we were, and it showed on his face and in his voice, sober and serious as he was.

That afternoon, Larry and I went home and worked outside, behind the house. Larry was doing some concrete work around our swimming pool, while I worked in the flower beds. The phone rang. It was a nurse, calling excitedly from five west. "What kind of Popsicle does Kathy like?" she asked.

"I guess I don't really know," I responded. "Why do you ask?"

"Well, she sure likes root-beer flavor!" the nurse answered. "Because she's eating one right now!"

"What in the world are you talking about?" I demanded.

The nurse explained, practically shouting over the phone in her excitement. She and another nurse had tied Kathy upright in a wheelchair, as Larry had done the previous afternoon, and had placed a Popsicle into her hand. Awkwardly, but quite deliberately, Kathy had raised it to her face and gotten it into her mouth. She had repeated the behavior several times. Kathy was eating a Popsicle!

Good-bye, backyard; hello, hospital! I yelled the news to Larry. He dropped his tools where he was standing and literally ran to the back door. We dashed to the showers, threw on our clothes, and pulled into the Scottsdale Memorial Hospital parking lot in what must have been record time. By the time we reached the fifth floor, Kathy's Popsicle-eating episode was already over. The nurses had been so pleased with their patient's feat that they had pushed Popsicles into her hand over and over, showing her off to everyone on five west. When we arrived, she was tired of Popsicles, or the neural connection that made it possible had lapsed, or something; in any event, try as we might, we could not get Kathy to perform. No matter: It was enough merely to look at her and know she had done it. There was no question about it, now, at least as far as we were concerned. Kathy *was* getting better. She had turned the corner, and recovery was now in sight.

That day, Kathy began opening her eyes and keeping them open for brief periods of time. Her eyes were, for the most part, unfocused and vacant, staring off into space. She had opened her eyes on several occasions earlier, but only in a reflexive, blinking manner. This time it was different. She seemed to be opening her eyes intentionally, both eyes together, and keeping them open for longer and longer periods of time. Soon she began to focus on objects, or track people visually, as they moved about the room. It was obvious that she was not merely raising her eyelids; she was actually seeing things, and what she looked at was registering in her brain. We began to ask her if she could see us, as we leaned over her bed. "Kathy, can you see Mommy?" I would pull her chin toward me, so that her open, glazed eyes stared at me. "Kathy, this is your mom. Can you see me?" And, ever so slightly, she would nod that she could.

Within two days, Kathy's eyes were starting to show a normal sleeping-waking cycle. She would open her eyes in the morning and keep them open most of the day. She still looked stuporous and glassy eyed, but she gradually was able to focus better and better. Her body movements were also rapidly becoming more purposeful and more frequent. (On one occasion, as a nurse bent over her bed to adjust her pillows, Kathy bit her on the ear.) She would reach out and touch people who stood close to her bed, squeezing them with a single hand, as if she were discovering for the first time how people feel. We had the sense that she wanted to communicate, though she could not yet talk. Her grunting and random vocalizations became more frequent, and apparently more intentional. New, progressive behaviors occurred almost every day during the next week. Once, as Larry and I stood together at her bedside, I asked her, "Kathy, do you know your dad? Can you point to your dad?" Slowly, carefully, her eyes moved back and forth, from me to him and back again. "If you can see your dad, point to him,

Kathy." And in a slight, shaky motion of the hand, she did.

Encouraged by the Popsicle incident, we began giving her things to eat. We put soft pieces of fruit or other foods in her hand, and she would feed herself. Sometimes her hand didn't find her mouth until the third or fourth try, so she always smeared more of the food onto her face than into her mouth. Those first feeding sessions were gooey messes, but she didn't seem to mind, and we loved it. We pracically wallowed in every minute of it.

Ten weeks after she lost contact with the world, it seemed as if Kathy Miller had come alive again.

Chapter Fourteen

BY THIS POINT, any reader who is the parent of a teenage son is wondering, *"What about Larry, Junior?"* One need not be a parent to suspect that events in the Miller household in the spring and summer of 1977 must have had a powerful impact on Kathy's older brother. (Barbara Miller calls her son Larry Don—or sometimes the more informal Sport—to distinguish him from his father.)

Larry Don was sixteen years old that spring: an attractive young man, trim and fine featured, with blonde hair, like his sister. In 1977, his major interests were baseball, cars, and rock music—a rather normal list for a teenage boy. He played varsity baseball at Chaparrel High School, and was quite a good pitcher. He earned average grades without trying very hard, and never had difficulty making a friend or finding a date when he wanted one.

Larry Don and Kathy had a good relationship. He was older enough to feel the normal, protective urges of a big brother, but close enough that they had their share of typical sibling squabbles. He teased her frequently, in the manner of a sixteen-year-old brother who is more comfortable expressing affection by teasing than by the simple declarative statement "I love you." He loved his little sister, of course, but what sixteen-year-old takes the time to think about that sort of thing, much less express it—even if he knew how to go about it? What sixteen-year-old realizes how fragile life can be? What teenager thinks his bright little sister will be reduced one afternoon to a coma patient?

The accident hit Larry Don hard. It was tough to handle, tough to understand, tough to know how to cope with endless week after week of not knowing if Kathy would ever again be around to pester. In the early days of Kathy's hospitalization, Larry Don visited faithfully, but he was usually silent. He didn't know what to say; he would sit by her bedside, often for long periods of time. Occasionally he would try to talk to her, sometimes he would cry; usually he would sit and hold her hand, just to be there. She had numerous abrasions—pavement burns—on her hands and arms, and Larry Don would sit for hours and rub a special vitamin-E cream into those spots. Kathy has no scars on those spots today. Often the tension of being by Kathy's bedside would get to him, and he would leave the room, not unlike his father, to roam the halls of the hospital.

Being the brother of a coma patient is not easy. Kathy's accident got a lot of attention in Scottsdale, and Larry Don was bombarded by questions about her at school, virtually every day. The pressure of those constant questions was compounded by the fact that there was rarely anything to report. There was that awful, sixty-day stretch when Kathy was doing no better, no worse—he had no changes at all to report, in answer to the questions. "How's your sister?" was the standard greeting from school friends. "How's Kathy doing?" And what does one say to such a question, well-meaning as it is? Eventually the challenge to respond seems not worth the effort, and the natural imiulse is to withdraw, to bail out, to avoid the questions and the pressure and the people.

A suburban teenager who can't cope with that kind of pressure has an easy out, today. He can find pot to smoke, pills to pop, booze to drink. It becomes far easier to skip classes and go out to the lake and drink beer with your buddies than to face people who want only to talk about your comatose kid sister.

For the parents, the net result of all this is another child to worry about, another set of problems to compound the medical ones. Nothing is more predictable than the clashes that occur between a father and his son, as the son becomes a man. There must inevitably be the test of wills, that painful tearing of the bond between any Senior and Junior. In that sense, the tension that developed between the two Miller men was not unusual; but it is difficult for a father to keep that perspective, when he is in the middle of it. All he can see is that while one child is desperately sick, the other is making matters worse by behaving badly. The son, on the other hand, is simply doing what he must do to fight his own private battles. And if the two truly, deeply love each other, as did Larry and Larry Don, the clash can indeed be a painful, agonizing one.

When Larry Don was not at the hospital, he was any number of other places, but most importantly, he was not with his parents, and he was not at home. The Millers insist they did not feel they were neglecting him during those months. "No, absolutely not," says Larry. "He didn't feel neglected, because he knew what was going on. He understood." And Larry Don agrees with that assessment. Still, the clock and the calendar make no allowances for emergencies; there are only so many hours, so many days. The attention of the Millers that spring and summer was absorbed by Kathy's struggle to survive, and that left little time for a growing teenage son, who had battles of his own to fight. "We were trying to have a feel for Larry Don," Barbara recalls. "We really did try to keep the communication strong. But, try as we might, we lost him during that time."

"Losing him" can be a relative thing, of course. The distance that developed between Larry Don and his parents in 1977, the sense of alienation, might in another household be regarded as routine; but in the Miller family, accustomed to harmony and close communication, it hung like a cloud. It became a second family crisis.

There is a hole in the wall of the family room at the Miller home. One night Larry and Larry Don were engaged in one of those father-son discussions, which escalated into an argument, then almost into a fight. In a moment of overwhelming frustration, Larry Don angrily challenged his father to hit him. Larry instead turned to the wall and punched it furiously. Larry is a large, strong man, and his fist drove right through the wall. It was the only blow struck that night, or any other night. But the hole is there as testimony to the ragged emotional edge to which the accumulated pressures had brought them.

Kathy Miller had been a sister Larry Don could be proud of. She was bright, popular, and pretty. When she hovered in the coma, he stood by her, wept for her, and in his own way, prayed for her.

That was one side of Larry Don. The other side was the headstrong, restless teenage boy who wrecked his car and skipped school and got high and came in late at night and found a hundred ways to break his parents' hearts.

The lesson, one must conclude, is that life goes on. Kathy's coma did not relieve the Millers from the challenges of rearing a teenage son. It would seem only fair that the trauma of Kathy's accident should, at the very least, exempt them from the additional burden of a son's growing pains. Life, unfortunately, has no such neatly compensating balances.

Chapter Fifteen

KATHY was coming home!

It was the first week of June 1977. From that first nod of her head, Kathy's responsiveness had developed with dramatic speed. She was now waking up each morning and going to sleep at night. She was able to focus her eyes on people and objects, to put soft foods into her own mouth, however awkwardly, and to point to things that she wanted. She soon began to point to her mouth when she was hungry or thirsty, and one of us would scurry to feed her. As she regained full consciousness, her other medical problems began to come under control. Her body temperature finally settled at a normal level.

Dr. Christensen agreed that Kathy was well enough to go home. Now that she was no longer unconscious and no longer had medical problems that required constant monitoring, her further recovery could occur as well at home as at the hospital. After a few weeks at home, depending on her rate of improvement, she could return to Scottsdale Memorial for a period of intensive rehabilitation treatment. So the decision was made, and Dr. Christensen instructed one of the nurses on five west to conduct training sessions to prepare me to take care of Kathy. I happily passed the word to Larry and Larry Don that Dr. Christensen had given his official okay, and we all three began preparing for the big event.

Our excitement somewhat obscured a fact that soon came forcibly to our attention: The Kathy we were bringing home only scantly resembled the Kathy who had lived with us before. At the time, we hardly stopped to think about that. It was enough that she was alive and awake and finally coming home. We had regarded the challenge of Kathy's coma as the big problem, assuming that her postcoma recovery would occur as a matter of course. Dr. Christensen had always been cautious in her prognosis. He had always prefaced every projection with the phrase, "If she comes out of the coma. . . ." Perhaps we had not listened carefully enough past those first seven words; perhaps we had too great a tendency to feel that, if she only awakened, everything would turn out all right.

Now she was awake, and we had nothing to divert our attention from the hard, cold facts of her condition. Kathy weighed a bare fifty-five pounds, exactly half her normal weight. She could not talk. She could not walk. She had no control of her bowels and bladder, and consequently wore diapers. She had the mental characteristics of an infant, unable to engage in anything approaching normal, adolescent intellectual activity. She had virtually no muscular control; in fact, she was unable even to sit upright in a wheelchair, unaided. When Dr. Bryant removed the cast from her right side, it revealed a badly mangled leg. What little muscle remained, had atrophied to an almost useless state, and it was difficult to look at that leg and believe that she would ever walk again.

Okay, those were the down-side facts. A healthy, vigorous teenager had run out the door in March, and we were wheeling in an invalid on a stretcher in June. We were realistic enough to face those facts. But there was another set of facts to consider, as well. There was the way God had constantly brought Kathy, step by step, from the edge of death to this condition. There was the feeling He had given, that things were going to work out. I had not surrendered that hope for three months; I certainly didn't intend to give up on Kathy now. As many times as God had spoken to me before, as many times as He had undergirded our family just when we needed Him most, He could do it that many times again in the future, and I believed He would.

Dr. Christensen emphasized a single point: Every new step Kathy took toward recovery could be her last. She was a long, long way from being the "reasonably normal kid" Larry had prayed for. She was making gradual progress toward full recovery, but there was no guarantee she would continue to do so. At any point, she might level off and simply not get any better. Some patients with brain injuries as severe as Kathy's die; some are permanently comatose; some awaken, but are barely more than vegetables; some regain partial intellectual and physical abilities. But very few make it all the way back. Only rarely does a patient with an injury so severe and a coma of such duration return to the life of a reasonably normal kid. We understood that. But we also understood that the things of the flesh can be overruled by the things of the Spirit. That is called a miracle, and what Kathy needed was a miracle. We believed in miracles.

* * * *

There was much to be done. For the first two weeks, I was to have no help at home with Kathy—our insurance did not pay for in-home nursing, and we simply didn't have the money, otherwise. I was learning that caring for an invalid without professional help required extensive preparations. I put in a stock of baby food and disposable diapers, purchased a commode specially made for invalids, and rented a hospital bed and wheelchair. We considered redecorating Kathy's bedroom as a welcome-home gesture, but a nurse advised us against it. "Keep everything as much as possible the way it was before the accident," she told me. "When she gets home, she'll be confused and disoriented. She will be grasping for familiar things, so it will be better not to redecorate."

As the day of Kathy's return approached, the tension within the family increased. We all were feeling the pressure of the impending change. For the past three months, our lives had revolved around that six-story building downtown called Scottsdale Memorial Hospital. There Kathy had been attended around the clock by the hospital staff, every body function monitored, all her special needs met with the use of sophisticated equipment and well-trained personnel. Now she was being discharged into our care. Whatever she needed, we would have to provide. How many people have ever seriously thought about what is involved in the twenty-four-hour care of an invalid? I had certainly never done so, and now I wondered if I were up to the task. *Do I know how to do this?* I worried. And my anxiety, my uncertainty in facing this unknown situation, was shared by Larry and Larry Don.

The big move was set for a Saturday morning. That Friday night, I had a family conference with my two men on the back porch. I had been meeting with the head nurse, the doctors, and the sociologist at the hospital, to prepare for Kathy's return. They had given me a sobering, almost grim assessment of what it would be like to bring home an infant; and what the chances were that she would ever be much better than she was at that time. It was distinctly possible, they had warned me, that we would be living with an invalid in the house permanently. She would be noisy and disruptive; she would not be pleasant to look at; she would have to be fed, diapered, carried from one part of the house to another. It would not be easy. The situation would place demands on all of us, and it might never change. That was a sobering message, and my men had to hear it. That Friday night on the back porch, I laid it out to them, just as it had been laid out to me.

They had never sat through a talk like that. When it was all over, they swallowed hard, then responded like champs. Larry, Jr., stubbornly insisted, "Well, we're not going to hide Kathy, and we're not going to be embarrassed by her, either."

Larry, of course, agreed. "I think we ought to put her right out in the middle of everything, and not apologize for her. We're going to bring her home, and she's going to be a different person from the Kathy we knew before. We believe she *will* get better, but in the meantime, this is what we've got to deal with. And we're going to do it. That's all there is to it!"

And so, the next morning, Kathy rejoined the family. An ambulance brought her, retracing the very route up Scottsdale Road that we had all traveled together on that dreadful afternoon so long before. It was a day of great excitement—in many ways, a day of victory. Whatever the future held, one thing was certain: Our daughter was alive, and she was home. For the moment, all the question marks disappeared, and there was room for little else but rejoicing in the Miller household.

One small incident marred the occasion, if only slightly. Kathy had a dog, a poodle named Bridget. She was an affectionate pet, unusually loyal to Kathy. Bridget would follow Kathy around the house, even sitting patiently outside the bathroom door when Kathy was inside. Bridget learned to wait by the side of the road for the school bus to appear each afternoon, noisily welcoming Kathy as she stepped off the bus. While Kathy was in the hospital, Bridget was subdued, as if she missed her. We often thought about how happy the little dog would be to see Kathy again.

But when Kathy returned, Bridget was afraid of her. Try as we might, we couldn't persuade the poodle even to approach her. To the pet, the girl we brought in on that stretcher was a strange, forbidding figure, in no way resembling her former friend called Kathy. As far as Bridget could tell, Kathy Miller still had not returned home. On a day of celebration, it was a small, poignant reminder.

Bridget's confusion was not enough, however, to dim the luster of Kathy's homecoming. Even if she was only a shell of her former self, we welcomed her home with praise to the Lord for bringing her back to us, plus a unanimous determination that, with God's help, we were going to help her get better again.

Chapter Sixteen

KATHY spent her first night in the rented hospital bed, in her own bedroom. While in bed, she wore a "posey," a device much like a straitjacket, which ties a patient to the sides of the bed, to prevent too much thrashing about.

In the middle of the night, we heard struggling sounds—grunting and moaning—from Kathy's room. Larry jumped out of bed and hurried down the hall to her room. She had somehow become tangled in the posey; it was wrapped over her head and around her neck. We had visions of Kathy strangling herself on that contraption during the night, and the next day we moved her. We got a large foam-rubber mat, placed it on the floor of the family room, and covered it with blankets, making one big pallet on the family-room floor. We "baby proofed" the room, made sure nothing was within reach that she might pull down on top of herself, and left her free to lie and flop around on the floor.

One of the first outward signs of improvement came in Kathy's speech. From the first few days, she would roll around on the floor and make noises. She was much like a baby in so many ways, and her vocalizing sounded remarkably like the sounds a baby makes before learning to talk. We would say words to her, naming simple objects like "chair" or "TV," and she would point to them. She got progressively better at this little game, but still was unable to say words herself. We weren't sure whether she could not think clearly enough, or if she was merely unable to produce the appropriate sounds. Like the parents of a growing baby, we were eager to hear her say her first word, and we did all we could to push her toward it.

One afternoon, Larry was sitting on the floor beside Kathy, massaging her gently, as he often did. He looked down at her and said, "Kathy, say *mama*." It was not the first time one of us had tried to coach her this way. Kathy stared back at at her father, no sign of recognition in her eyes.

"Say *mama*, Kathy," he repeated softly. Still no answer—just that glazed, empty stare.

Larry persisted. "Come on, Kathy. Do it for me, honey. Just say *mama*!" And this time, unmistakably in response to his words, Kathy pressed her lips together and formed the word with her mouth. But no sound came out. She did it again and again, mouthing the word mutely as she looked up at Larry, until finally a faint sound came out.

"That's right, Kathy. Try it again!"

And the next time, it was a full, clear word: "Mama," said Kathy Miller.

Larry jumped up from the floor and ran to get me. I hurried to the family room, and Kathy rewarded me with several more "mamas." She spoke with a toneless, flat, mechanical voice, but a more beautiful "mama" I have never heard in my life! We tried "daddy" after that, and with a bit of effort got her to repeat that word, then "Kathy." That went on for several days; she soon graduated to three- or four-word sentences. We would say them slowly to her, and she seemed to take pleasure in repeating them back to us: "Kathy is great. Kathy is pretty. Kathy is fantastic." The words were repeated in a monotone, with no inflection or expression (a common problem of brain-damaged patients, which we had been told to expect), but it was great progress, nonetheless.

We could only hope that this small step was not the last one, as the hospital staff had warned might be the case. We really didn't worry about that, at the time. For the moment, we were determined to do everything we could to give Kathy a chance. We knew that she had always been a very stubborn, determined little girl, and we believed that her great spirit was still alive within her. Somewhere, down inside that damaged body, was the Kathy whom the Dominicans had called Betola. Somewhere down there was the Kathy who hated to lose on that tough fourth lap of those mile races. We didn't want to push her too hard or expect too much, but we felt that we owed it to her to give her every chance to fight her way back.

This attitude of ours was part of the decision to put Kathy into the swimming pool at our house as early as we did. We had asked the doctors about putting Kathy into the water as soon as possible when we got her home, and they had discouraged the idea, feeling it was much too early for that. But I prayed about it, and I felt that God was telling me to put her into the water. Since the doctors had not absolutely forbidden it, we decided to give it a try. The second night she was home was a typically hot, June night. We thought maybe the pool would cool her down, and we wanted to see how she would react to the water. The hot weather was all the excuse we needed.

Larry picked Kathy up in his arms and stepped into the water. The cool water on her legs frightened her. She grabbed Larry's neck tightly, as he carried her into deeper water. That first night he just walked around the pool with Kathy in his arms. He did it again the next night, and the next. She came to enjoy it; she liked the feel of the water on her body. After several days, we put a life jacket on her and let her float, as we pulled her around the pool. She began to give little kicking motions as we did so, and we were delighted to see that the motions of swimming were still stored somewhere in her brain. We began to hold her upright in the water and stand her on her feet. I would hold her in that position, as Larry held her hands and pulled her toward himself. The water buoyed her up, bearing the weight of her body. As Larry pulled her slowly toward him, she moved her legs slightly, one after the other, in a motion much like walking.

All these events were the cause of much rejoicing and praising God at our house. It took very little in those days to excite us. Even though Kathy had almost no muscle tone and was unable to walk on her own, we felt that her behavior in the water was an indication that the brain was still sending the right signals to her legs; sooner or later, we felt, the rest would come. We spent time in the pool every day.

The summer dragged along. It often seemed that each small step forward was followed by another period of disappointment and doubt. The ordeal was hardest on Larry. One night I went to the bedroom and found Larry already in bed. When he turned toward me, his eyes were red, and it was obvious he had been crying. My heart went out to him. "Do you want to talk about it?" I asked him. That time, he did. Usually so private with his feelings, so determined not to show what he thought might be seen as weakness, that night he let it all out. He was under pressure from his job, frustrated and unhappy, bills were piling up, and not enough money was coming in to stay even. He was putting himself down for all that.

"Look," he said, "let's look at it honestly. I'm in debt. I feel frustrated in my job. I've got a daughter who may never be normal again. I've got a son, and I don't know where his head is. I don't know why he's doing what he's doing, and somehow I feel responsible. . . ."

I interrupted him right there. "Let me tell you what I see, Larry," I said. "I see a guy who is in his early forties, in the prime of life. He is a terrific husband and father. He has learned how to love people, learned what are the really important things in life. Money's not a big deal. We've made money before; we can make it again. As far as Larry Don is concerned, he might be having a rough time now, but we've committed that to God, and it's going to improve. And I'm not even going to accept what you're thinking about Kathy. That's the most ridiculous thing I've ever heard. If someone had told you two months ago that Kathy would be alive and awake and at home right now, you wouldn't have believed it was possible. So if God has brought her this far, we can be sure He's got a plan for her future."

That wasn't just a pep talk for Larry. I believed every word of it, and I wanted so much for Larry to be able to believe it as strongly as I did.

* * * *

None of us will ever forget Kathy's first spontaneously spoken sentence. Her verbal behavior had been gradually improving; within a couple of weeks, she was saying random, single words. She had progressed beyond mere repetition of words spoken to her, but still was not putting words together into sentences, without coaching. Her first spontaneous sentence was

another of those firsts that God gave to Larry. He recalls the occasion: "We were sitting out on the patio,
around the pool, late one night. It was just the two of
us. I was sitting there, just looking at Kathy in her
wheelchair. Those were times of tremendous anxiety
for me; I had no idea what her chances of total rehabilitation really were.

"As I sat looking at Kathy, she opened her mouth
and spoke, as plainly as can be. It wasn't a grunt or a
word. She said to me: 'All I need is time.' I couldn't
believe it! Until then, she had only said an isolated
word or two, or mimicked someone else. She said it
again: "All I need is time." It was slow and slurred,
but there was absolutely no mistaking what she said! I
ran into the house to tell Barb, and she came back outside and sat with us, and we gave thanks for that message from God. That's what I believe it was. To my
knowledge, we had never used that phrase around
Kathy before, so I don't think she had picked it up that
way. I believe God was speaking to me through her.
That was the first real revelation to me that maybe
Kathy was going to be okay. Until then, I was just sort
of holding on and hoping. But that night I really began
to believe that maybe she was going to make it."

* * * *

It was important for us not to let ourselves compare
Kathy with the way she had been before the accident.
As long as we compared her with where she had been
a week or a month earlier, we could see progress and
keep our spirits high.

Day by day, she regained the use of her body. After that first sentence on the patio that night, her verbal ability increased rapidly. She also began to gain weight. She was still unable to eat solid foods, so we fixed all sorts of high-calorie concoctions in the blender for her. Larry would pick her up in his arms and stand on the bathroom scale to check her weight, and after a few days at home, it began to edge upward again.

After a few weeks at home, we took her back to the hospital, to see Dr. Christensen. She was sitting up in her wheelchair, unaided, when we wheeled her into his office, and he could hardly believe his eyes. He jumped up from behind his desk to take a closer look. He was so pleased with her progress that he directed us to check her into the hospital immediately, to begin a two-week rehabilitation program.

During that two weeks, we missed Kathy more than ever. After the first few days, we talked with Dr. Peter Ortiz, her rehabilitation specialist, about bringing her home to visit each day. He agreed that we could bring her home every afternoon, if we would have her back at the hospital by 9:30 each evening. We eagerly agreed. We had a prize daughter and hated to give her up. We savored every moment of those visits and stretched the time as far as we could. We got her back to Scottsdale Memorial at 9:30 the first time, then at 9:45, then 10:15. It was difficult to let her go. She loved pralines and ice cream, so we went by the ice-cream shop every night, on the way to the hospital. Those were great times.

After two weeks, Kathy came home from the hospital for the second time. She would be going back for regular rehabilitation treatments on an outpatient basis, but otherwise, she was being discharged to our care; the hospital staff had done all they could for her. From now on, whatever progress she made was up to her and the good Lord.

Chapter Seventeen

IT HAD BEEN a dreadful day. It was a hot, summer afternoon in Phoenix, one of those days when everything that can possibly go wrong does.

The temperature outside hovered between 105 and 110 degrees. The washer-dryer broke down. The car wouldn't start and had to be fixed. Worse yet, the air-conditioning system in our house broke down, and on a Phoenix summer day, that is no small problem. I was frustrated and irritable, and so was Larry. We decided to check into a motel for the night, while the air conditioning was being repaired. The house was a hotbox, so I wheeled Kathy outside and left her sitting in her wheelchair by the side of the car, in the cooler shade of the carport, while Larry and I got our things together to leave for the motel.

As I scurried around the house, the doorbell rang. A bit exasperated at this interruption, I went to answer it.

I opened the front door, and there, to my utter amazement, stood Kathy! I was stunned! She just stood there, with that almost expressionless look, only the faintest bit of a grin on her face.

I recovered my composure and exclaimed, "Kathy, that's fantastic!" She still stood there, as if she were basking in the moment. "Kathy, I've got an idea," I said. "Let's see if you can do it again!" She made no sign of protest, so with that, I walked her slowly back over to the wheelchair, which was still parked beside the car, and put her into it. "Let's see if you can do it again, Kathy!" I repeated, then went back inside the house. I sat down in the living room and waited, glued to the chair, praying to hear that doorbell ring again. I waited. Three minutes went by, then four and five. It seemed like an eternity. I had to force myself to stay in the chair. Eight minutes, nine minutes . . . and then the doorbell rang!

This time I ran—not to the door, but to the kitchen, to get Larry. I practically dragged him to the front door, ignoring his questions, threw the door open, and there, triumphantly, stood Kathy. We asked her to do it one more time, this time while we watched, to see how she was managing such a feat. She had reached from her wheelchair, grabbed the door handle of the car, and pulled herself to her feet. Then, leaning against the car, she made her way along it, to the front fender, which was only a few feet across the driveway from the doorpost. She traveled those few feet on her own, lurching across to grab the post before losing her balance. From there, only a single step was required to reach the doorbell. Larry and I watched as she made that short, excruciating journey for the third time that afternoon.

And so, in that fashion, Kathy walked her first steps since March. In her typically independent, determined way, she had done what so many people thought she would never do again. It was a start, and she made great improvement after that, walking more frequently, for longer distances without tiring, with less and less of the awkward, lurching movements of a cripple.

Her use of her arms and hands also improved. After Kathy began talking, it occurred to us to place a pen in her hand, put paper in front of her, and urge her to try to write something. It was a shaky, barely controlled hand that moved the pen, but her brain was obviously sending the correct signals, even if the muscle control was poor. She finally managed to put a sprawling, spidery scrawl on the paper. The crude letters were barely discernible; but, when we looked closely, we could read her message: "Kathy is great!"

From the beginning of her recovery, she had a severe tremor in her right hand. She couldn't pick up a glass of water, without sloshing it around. We tried to let her do as many things as possible; as a result, there were lots of broken dishes around our kitchen and dining room that summer and fall. (Eventually her lack of control of the right hand would force us to shift her from being a right-handed person to a left-handed one.) Kathy's brain had to relearn those things that we take so much for granted. She had to practice, hour after hour, to learn to do the simple things that come easily to normal persons. We worked with her, helping develop her sense of depth and distance, her eye-hand coordination, and her basic body balance. We would work with her on the floor, playing with children's toys, stacking and unstacking ABC blocks, and rolling rubber balls back and forth across the floor. Slowly, she made progress.

Through all of this, Kathy proved to be a girl with lots of old-fashioned courage. She was willing to struggle, even to hurt, if that was required, in order to get better. Larry and I often marveled at her tenacity and sometimes wondered how she could maintain such a fighting heart. Over the years we had funneled into our children lots of positive thinking and a never-say-die spirit, part of the attitudes we had developed in our Amway business, and we feel that perhaps some of that surfaced in Kathy's virtually instinctive response to the challenges she confronted.

At the root of it all was something bigger and stronger than merely a positive mental attitude, however. The source of Kathy's real strength was the same thing that had kept us going during the ten weeks of her coma: It was the assurance that God had His hand on her shoulder. We told Kathy, "When you get discouraged, just think the word *Jesus*, and think about what it means." She understood what trusting God was about. She adopted a slogan: "I can do anything, with God's help." She would repeat that, in her determined monotone, over and over, as she tried to walk or swim or feed herself.

Kathy began talking about running. At first, she mentioned it casually, but gradually it became a major issue with her—she wanted to run again. At this time, she was walking, although rather stiffly. Even though she was still very unstable, with poor balance and overall lack of muscle control, at least she could walk. But run? That was something else.

Dr. Christensen had warned us that, as Kathy improved mentally, she would become more and more aware of her physical problems and correspondingly more despondent and frustrated by them. By the end of the summer, she was reaching that point. Mentally, she was becoming more alert, and that served to make her physical rehabilitation seem even slower to her.

As Kathy grew increasingly discontented with herself, I prayed for God to show us a way to keep her from the negative thoughts that seemed to be growing inside her. One day she was doing what we call "counting the empties"—talking about the things she could *not* do, rather than emphasizing those things that she *could* do. I stopped her right on the spot, and we bowed our heads and prayed for God to teach us how to maintain a better attitude, to show us an alternative to "counting the empties."

I felt, as I prayed, that God wanted us to set a goal, something specific to work toward, which would keep our minds on "can do" rather than "can't do." So

I asked Kathy, "What single thing would you like to be able to do again that you could do before the accident?"

Kathy answered without a moment's hesitation. "Run," she said. "I want to run."

"Okay, we're going to run," I told her. "Let's go get our running stuff on." She gave me an incredulous look, saw that I was serious, and we got up and headed for our bedrooms, to put on our jogging outfits. Within twenty minutes, we were dressed and ready to go. We drove to Cocopah elementary school and parked near the running track. It was late afternoon. We got out of the car and walked onto the track. It was the standard 440 yards around, but that day it looked like 4 miles. I breathed a little prayer, and we started to run.

At first, we would jog one or two steps, then walk eight or ten, then jog another step or two, and so on. It actually was not running—not even jogging, that first time. What Kathy did was more of a shuffle. I could hear her bad right foot dragging behind, and all I could think was *Praise the Lord!* I wasn't thinking about how pitifully she was shuffling along; my mind and heart were too full of joy at hearing the sound of my Kathy running! *How far we've come from that bed in the Scottsdale Memorial ICU!* I thought. The sound of that dragging right foot was a wonderful, joyful sound to me.

We only "ran" about fifty yards that first day. It was painful for Kathy, and she was exhausted and panting after we had gone that far. We stopped, and right there, in the Cocopah school yard, we prayed a prayer of thanks. We both believed that Kathy was going to run again, as a symbol of her recovery and as a witness to the healing power of a loving God. It was a small start, but it was a start, nonetheless.

We ran every day, after that. Gradually the distances lengthened. One day we had gone about three-quarters of the way around the track, our farthest distance yet. Kathy was exhausted and slightly palefaced. "Do you want to stop, Kathy?" I asked her.

"No," she panted back to me. "I want to finish."

And so, that afternoon we finished one complete lap around the track—one-quarter mile. Not long afterward, we stopped going to the Cocopah track and began running instead on the empty fairways of the Scottsdale Country Club golf course. Larry frequently joined us. As Kathy's distances increased, so did her stride. She had once been such a graceful, fluid runner, with a beautiful, strong stride, and now she ran like an awkward colt. That clumsiness bothered her, and she worked to strengthen her right leg and run more evenly.

To us, Kathy's running was a meaningful breakthrough: If she could run, other types of progress were also possible. And to Kathy, too, running became an important symbol. To her, it was a symbol of full recovery, an affirmation that Kathy Miller was back in action, that she was once again a fully functioning part of the world. "It was particularly important, to me, to run again," Kathy explains today. "I just felt I had to. I enjoyed it so much before the accident, I felt I had to run again. I can't tell you how important it was to me, not just to run, but to run well."

Chapter Eighteen

KATHY would run again, and run well. Her running would bring public acclaim and would be a source of inspiration to people around the world. But not yet. Before any of that would happen, before the miracle of Kathy Miller's recovery would be complete, there were a hundred other problems to be solved, countless other challenges to be met.

One of the toughest of these was the problem of getting back into school. Kathy had been injured in early spring, but she had been allowed to graduate from elementary school on schedule, along with her eighth-grade class. She had the entire spring and summer to recover, but the next fall, she was still unprepared to return to a regular classroom. Remarkable as her progress had been, she was still far from recovering the intellectual ability she had before the accident. She was bravely moving toward a normal life, but it could not happen overnight.

As Kathy gained better control of her body and speech in the early autumn of 1977, she hoped for a normal re-entry into the mainstream of her ninth-grade class. Such a hope was rather naive, given the extent of the damage she had suffered, and Dr. Christensen, as usual, had the unhappy task of telling her so. In a visit to his office shortly before the opening of school, she expressed to him her desire to return to a regular classroom. Gently, but quite firmly, he explained to her the sad facts: She was testing below the first-grade level on some mental tests and at the second- and third-grade level on others. She still suffered from severe aphasia (an inability to engage in normal verbal activity). She had major memory deficits, and had serious problems with short-term memory (she might be told something and forget it within a minute or less). She clearly was not ready for the normal academic demands of the ninth grade.

Kathy was upset by Dr. Christensen's blunt appraisal of her condition. She had invested so much effort and pain into her physical rehabilitation, and was making great progress in that area; now her doctor was telling her she had the same exhausting process ahead in the mental and cognitive area. "You're getting better, Kathy," he told her, "but it takes time. Even for you, it takes time. Your brain must learn lots of things all over again, and it is no different from any other part of your body. You're just going to have to work at it and hope for the best."

And so she did. After the shock of hearing that she

was to be a special-education student, Kathy plunged into the job of making herself better. She was assigned to the learning-resource center, a special unit for children with learning disabilities at Chaparral High School. She went to work with the same gritty determination that carried her around the running track every afternoon. Her family helped. Larry and Barbara Miller bought coloring books and early childhood math and spelling books, and patiently worked with Kathy for hours, every day after school. While they worked with her, they constantly reminded her of what was good about her situation—constantly emphasized the positive, the hopeful, the good.

Kathy's schoolwork early that year resembled the work of a first grader. She did the most elementary things, the things one learns at age seven or eight, then slowly built on that restored foundation, back toward where she had been before the injury. She had to learn to read all over again, making her way through the "Look and See" books from which kindergarteners study. Learning to write was an even greater struggle; Kathy's cognitive disability, combined with her lack of muscular control, made legible writing virtually impossible. Developing a firm, readable penmanship would eventually require hundreds of hours of practice.

After half a year at the learning-resource center, Kathy was moved to the special-education class of Scottsdale High School for the second semester of the 1977–78 school year. She was still not capable of a conventional academic load, but she was getting closer. "It was pretty hard," she recalls. "I had to study more than I ever did before, and I had to work hard, just to learn how to do the simplest little things. My speech and my writing really got on my nerves. Sometimes I know words that fit what I'm trying to say, but I can't think of them. Everything seems to take a little more work, but it's getting easier. I'm making my comeback."

Kathy's academic challenges were matched by difficulties on the social scene. A big part of her comeback effort involved the process of adjusting to a new set of friends, following an absence of several months. She also had to cope with the fact that she looked and behaved somewhat differently from before.

When she first returned to school, Kathy's eyes still looked glazed, and she walked awkwardly. Many of her schoolmates thought she was on drugs, and would ask her brother, Larry, Jr., who was at the same school that year, "Is your sister stoned again?" At that age, friendships rarely are durable enough to withstand long separations, and Kathy returned to school to find most of her old friends involved in new interests. Being in the special-education program further removed her from them, and Kathy's social activity, like so much else, was largely a matter of starting life over again.

Kathy was keenly aware of the differences. "Let's face it, I was weird. I *was* different. I was afraid to face up to my friends, because I was so different. I felt like a kindergartener among all these 'grown-up' high-school kids."

Nor did Kathy fit with the average special-ed students. She was placed among retarded children and those with permanent disabilities. The more her own condition improved, the less well she related to them and the more frustrated she became by the situation. She was in a kind of social limbo, unable during that year to find real acceptance, either from her fellow special-ed students or from the regular Scottsdale High kids. It was a tough situation for a sensitive young girl. She would come home from school, day after day, at the point of tears—or past it. She and Barbara would talk, then they would pray. It was the same formula as always for them: lots of talking it out, then lots of prayer, then a conscious, determined attempt to look on the positive side of things.

Barbara suggested, on one such occasion, that Kathy begin an all-out effort to bridge the social gap between herself and the other special-ed kids. "You're more advanced than they are, Kathy," she told her, "so you've got to take the lead. You've got to go out of your way to *make somebody else feel good.*" They decided to call these gestures of goodwill "warm fuzzies." Kathy would get credit for one warm fuzzy each time she said something or did something to make someone else feel good. There were two requirements for an act to qualify as a warm fuzzy: It must be sincere and it must be done or said without expecting anything in return. Kathy made a mark on her hand with a ball-point pen each time she scored a warm fuzzy, and when she got home each afternoon, she and her mother transferred the marks to a special calendar they hung on the wall.

It made quite a difference. Rather than coming home from school to cry on Barbara's shoulder, Kathy was coming home to rack up her warm-fuzzy points. The social chemistry began to change for Kathy, and as it did, her own positive nature had more room to oper-ate. (Kathy still keeps that old calendar from the winter and spring of 1978. Her all-time record high was eigh-teen warm fuzzies in a day.)

As the year progressed, Kathy improved in every area. She was Scottsdale's version of the unsinkable Molly Brown. One day that spring, she arose early, as usual, to practice her handwriting before going off to school. It was April of 1978. A year earlier, she had been in what was thought to be an irreversible coma. A postscript on a scrap of paper from her alphabet prac-tice on that typical morning speaks volumes about the spirit of Kathy Miller:

6:30 A.M.   Kathy Miller
                            4/3/78

Aa Bb Cc Dd Ee Ff Gg Hh Ii
Jj Kk Ll Mm Nn Oo Pp Qq
Rr Ss Tt Uu Vv Ww Xx
Yy Zz

         P.T.L.
            today's going to be
         another butiful day!

Chapter Nineteen

WHEN WE BEGAN jogging, it was beyond our wildest dreams that Kathy's running would someday draw so much attention. I was simply trying to pull her attention away from her disabilities and focus instead on the things she could do.

I firmly believed in the slogan Kathy was using: "With God's help, I can do anything!" I wanted to show her just how true it is, so when she told me that the thing she wanted to do more than anything else was to run again, it seemed a good place to put our faith to the test. As we started running, even though it was slow and clumsy, it was immediately apparent that this was something Kathy enjoyed. She loved it—even the difficult times, the painful times. It was a natural thing, I suppose, when one considers how much she had enjoyed competitive running before the accident, but I was amazed at the degree to which running became, to her, such an important symbol of her personal comeback. A few weeks after our running began, an accident occurred that might have ended the whole thing right there.

Larry had left town on a business trip, and Kathy and I decided to run that day on the street that fronts our house. It was a foolish thing to do, as I later realized, but at the time, I was simply trying to save the time of driving to the Cocopah school grounds. We were running along slowly, Kathy behind me, and I glanced back over my shouder, to see how she was doing. I looked back just in time to see her fall. She went down heavily, flush on her face. Her coordination was too poor and her arms too weak to break her fall, so she took the blow entirely on her shoulder and face.

As I bent over her, I saw fear in her face, and for a moment her fear swept over me, as well. Her face was bloody, and the sight of the blood made me momentarily nauseous. I had a sickening flashback to the accident; the image of Kathy's crumpled body in Scottsdale Road came flashing into my mind. I was scared, and I prayed: "Lord, take all the fear from both of us—right now, Lord—and help us to do the right thing." The fear passed. I helped Kathy to her feet, and we made it back to the house.

I packed Kathy's face with ice and called the doctor. He reassured me that any neurological complications were unlikely, and told me to bring her in, to have her checked over. The X rays showed a fractured nose, but he said it should heal itself. "If not," he said, "we'll know within ten days, and we'll have to break it again and reset it. But I think it will heal properly without that." Kathy knew what to do about that. "Let's just claim it from the Lord!" she suggested, and that's what we did. The morning after the fall, her eyes were swollen shut and her face was badly bruised, but the nose did heal in place, and there was no need to treat it afterward.

Larry and I feared the trauma of that fall might destroy Kathy's desire to run, but it hardly seemed to affect her at all. Within a week we were at it again, though this time we ran along the soft fairways of a nearby golf course, just in case she fell again.

One day that autumn, I told one of our business associates about Kathy's running, and how much it was helping her, and mentioned that I felt she needed some goal to work toward in her running, something specific to shoot for. "I think I know just the thing," he told me, mentioning the North Bank Run. It was a 10,000-meter race through the Phoenix suburbs, and it was to be a major event, drawing several thousand runners. "Why not suggest it to Kathy as a goal?" he asked. "Not to win, or even to finish, but just to give it a try."

I talked it over with Larry, and he said, "Why not?" He, too, felt that Kathy needed a goal, something to stretch toward, something she could really feel good about. He talked it over with Kathy. What did she think? "Good goal," answered Kathy. Just like that.

Ten-thousand meters is 6.2 miles, and as we worked to build up our stamina over the next few weeks, we talked more and more about not merely running, but making a real effort to finish the entire distance. All I could think about, as I listened to Kathy talk, was how great it would be for her morale and self-confidence, if somehow she could pull it off and finish that 10,000 meters.

The North Bank Run was on a Sunday, a crisp November day. We arrived at the starting point, Larry, Kathy, and I, about an hour early. We signed up, got our numbers, and took our place among the thousands of other runners. When the starting gun sounded, we were off and running, amidst much pushing and jostling of all those bodies. We ran slowly, and the serious competitive runners soon were far ahead. We drew lots of stares from the spectators; Kathy was still running awkwardly at that stage, and people who saw her must have wondered why a girl in her condition would be out there at all. A few of them jeered. Kathy seemed not to notice; she was intent on a single thing, and that was finishing the race.

The six miles started at the corner of Camelback and Fortieth Street, passed through a residential area, alongside a canal to the Biltmore Country Club, then back up the other side of the canal to the finish line. After two miles, Kathy was tired and perspiring. She kept on. After four miles, she was limping, favoring her right leg. She kept on running. Her speed slowed to a virtual crawl. She was hurting in a dozen places—but when the six-mile point was passed and the FINISH banner came into view, stretched across the road up ahead, Kathy still had something in reserve, more than she realized. She finished, and she finished running! No matter that the field had finished far ahead of her, that she had limped and struggled much of the way. She was not running this race to win; she was running this race to finish, and finish she did!

It was a statement: Hello, world—Kathy's back! And she learned something, too, that day. She learned that she had it in her to accomplish anything she set out to do which required will and determination and endurance. She learned that nothing is impossible. If a fourteen-year-old girl can run and finish a 10,000-meter race within 6 months of being deep in a coma, what other miracles might be out there waiting?

* * * *

Kathy's participation in the North Bank Run triggered a remarkable chain of events, which ultimately enabled her to testify to God's power before a worldwide audience.

A reporter for the Arizona *Republic* was there that day, and wrote a front-page article about her courageous run. The AP and UPI wire services picked up the story, and it ran in newspapers across the country. The *Los Angeles Times* version of the story was seen by a representative of the Victoria Sporting Club, an organization in London, England, which annually selects the world's most courageous athlete. The award given by this organization is called the International Award for Valour in Sport. Within a few weeks of the North Bank Run, we were notified that Kathy had been nominated for this award for 1978.

The odds against her receiving the award were long. There were 800 nominees, from 120 countries. Most of them were exceptional athletes, such as pitcher Tommy John (then of the Los Angeles Dodgers) and American jockey Steve Cauthen. The previous year, the award had been won by Niki Lauda, the famous Austrian race car driver. The idea of a nonprofessional, unknown teenager from Arizona winning the award seemed preposterous.

Those were the odds, but I had another input. From the first mention of the award, I had a clear impression that Kathy would win it—not just be a finalist, though that would be remarkable enough—but win it outright. I shared my input with Larry, and he cautioned me not to get my hopes up prematurely. But I felt it so strongly that, in December, when I mailed out our annual mimeographed newsletter to all our relatives and friends, I said so: "The top ten nominees are flown to London. . . . I believe Kathy will be among those top ten. In fact, I have the same calm . . . knowledge I had at the accident that God is the Victor, and Kathy will be the recipient of the award next February. It will be fun for you to read this later. . . ." I really don't know why I had the gall to write such a confident prediction two months before it came to pass, except that I felt God had spoken to me. (Larry told me he hoped I was keeping a list of everyone to whom I sent the newsletter, so I could write back later, to retract!)

God was going to allow Kathy to receive this award, so that He could receive the glory. He would do it as a means of witnessing of His love for Kathy and all the other Kathys in this world. I believed that as strongly as I had believed God was taking care of her all through her coma. He would give her the award, and she would witness to His love.

And it unfolded, all of it, in just that way. In late December, we were notified that Kathy was a finalist. We were flown to England in February, all four of us, and treated like royalty. We met the other finalists and many famous athletes from around the world. The night before the award ceremony, Larry crawled into bed with me in our London hotel room, gave me a big grin, and said, "Okay, now. What are you going to do if she doesn't win?"

I didn't ever have to answer that question. The next day, the four of us sat in the crowded Great Guildhall in London and listened as Kathy's name was called as the winner of the award. The solid-gold medal was presented to her by His Royal Highness Prince Michael of Kent, while an orchestra of the Welsh Color Guard played and a live television audience of millions of viewers watched. Larry and I could only sit and marvel at where God had brought us. Several months earlier, if someone had told us that our daughter would one day be in such a place, receiving such an award for such an accomplishment, we couldn't have even imagined it. It would have been beyond our biggest dreams. But there she was, in testimony to the way God's plans for us can be far greater than even our own best hopes. And when Kathy stepped to the microphone to accept the award, her voice, still slow and slurred from her injuries, expressed exactly what I was feeling.

"Most of all," she said, "I'd like to thank the good Lord for, you know, keeping me alive and helping me through it all. I'm just here to be His representative."

Amen! And praise the Lord!

Epilogue

KATHY MILLER has continued to be His representative since that day, and to a far larger audience than on that occasion.

She returned to Scottsdale after that ceremony and, in the first Sunday service after arriving home, dedicated her winning medal to God on the altar of the Scottsdale United Methodist Church.

Subsequently, more acclaim has come her way. The Arizona Marathon Society has established an award for their Most Courageous Runner, to be given annually in Kathy's honor at the North Bank Run. The Philadelphia Sports Writers Association selected her as the Most Courageous Athlete in America for 1979. She threw out the first balls on the opening-night games of the 1979 season for both the Los Angeles Dodgers and the Atlanta Braves. She has flown to Belfast, Ireland, to appear at a track meet with Olympic-gold-medal winner Mary Peters. She was recently hosted at a White House reception by President Carter's wife, Rosalynn.

Back home, Kathy's remarkable comeback has continued. She is now sixteen years old, and is a regular student at Scottsdale Christian Academy. She is a high-school junior, and hopes to go on to study fashion design after she graduates. The effect of her injury still appears in slightly slower speech, but the spontaneity and inflection has long since returned to her voice, and the expression to her face. She admits that schoolwork is harder than it was before; she studies hard now to make C+s or Bs in courses that at one time yielded easy As.

Kathy's leg is now fully functional, and plastic surgery has done much to reduce its badly scarred appearance of a year ago. According to her orthopedic surgeon, the leg "does all the things a leg is designed to do."

Barbara Miller has also been honored for her part in Kathy's comeback. She was selected as the Arizona Mother of the Year in 1979 by the American Mothers Committee, and was nominated for the national award by that same organization.

Larry, Jr., has graduated from Scottsdale High School, and is now living at home with his family and is a full-time college student. Larry resigned from his job with the Portland Cement Association; he is now serving as marketing director for a Phoenix consulting engineering firm, as well as helping to manage the family's Amway business.

Dr. Fred Christensen, to most people a hero in Kathy's comeback, still insists that he deserves no applause for his role, that he only did his job with a girl who has been very fortunate to recover as she has. He continues to work with brain-damage cases at Scottsdale Memorial Hospital. Why? "Look, somebody has to do something," he said recently. "The problem doesn't go away. In the past, none of these kids went home. You put them in a nursery someplace, and all they got was bedsores and pneumonia. The fact is that we send them home a lot better than they would be otherwise. That's all."

Dr. Jack Jewell, still practicing medicine in the Phoenix area, reflects on the experience: "I think it's a miracle. From the medical standpoint, from the amount of damage, her improvement is remarkable. Who would ever have dreamed it would have been possible?"

Who, indeed? The mysteries of life and death, of suffering and recovery, are beyond human intelligence. No individual, however great his faith or close his walk with God, can guarantee that tragedy will not strike or death will not call. There are many Kathys, many pretty schoolgirls, each of them someone's daughter, who arrive at emergency wards each year. Many do not survive; many others never recover from their injuries. Larry and Barbara Miller, as they tell their story, emphasize that its real message is that God's presence makes a difference *under any circumstances*. Barbara felt that God's peace was given to her in answer to prayer; she believed that, even if Kathy died, somehow things, in her phrase, "would be all right."

It is that unshakable sense of the loving presence of God that was Barbara Miller's gift: the faith that God knows us, loves us, and somehow will make the events in our lives—all of them, however tragic they seem—work together to our ultimate benefit. That faith meets needs of every type; it overcomes obstacles of every description. That faith, and the great loving God on which it rests, is the theme of this story.

Kathy Miller, as she declares, is only His representative.